Valerie Grimwood

Starting Needlepoint Lace

A course for beginners

B. T. Batsford Ltd · London

Frontispiece: Venetian Gros Point lace (sixteenth century); photograph taken by Mrs Susan Cox of a piece of lace from the Dr A. I. Spriggs Collection which is housed and looked after by the English Lace School.

© Valerie Grimwood 1989
First published 1989
First paperback edition 1995
Reprinted 2000

ISBN 0 7134 5807 0

Typeset by Keyspools Ltd, Golborne, Warrington
and printed in Spain by Bookprint, S.L., Barcelona
for the publishers
B.T. Batsford Ltd
9 Blenheim Court
Brewery Road
London N7 9NT

A member of the Chrysalis Group plc

To Nenia Lovesey
who has done so much to stimulate and encourage the spread of
needlepoint lace

Contents

Acknowledgements **8**

Foreword **9**

Introduction **11**

1 Equipment **13**

2 Stages in working **17**

3 Making a simple motif **42**

4 More stitches and 'sampler' projects **66**

5 Decorative finishes **95**

6 Design, colour and threads **115**

Suppliers **122**

Further reading **126**

Index **127**

Acknowledgements

I would like to thank everyone who has taught me needlepoint lace, thus giving me so much pleasure and without whom this book would not have been possible: especially Mary Anderson (who started me off), Catherine Barley (who also kindly read through the manuscript), Doreen Holmes and Carol Williamson. Also my thanks to Iris Farrington for her expert photography; Carol Mathews for the typing; Alexandra Stillwell for her inestimable help and encouragement; Susan Cox of the English Lace School for the use of the Venetian lace photograph; Shirley Osborne for letting me use the idea in the Guild of Needlelace's magazine for making a polystyrene pillow; Irene Day for working the lace mat.

My grateful thanks to Nenia Lovesey for her interest in my lacemaking and kindness in writing the foreword of this book. Last, but not least, a thank you to my husband and daughter for putting up with my continued obsession with lace!

Foreword

This book has been written for the lacemakers who are far away from the help of a tutor, and also for those who say that they have difficulty in following written instructions.

The instructions in this book are so clear, that they could turn an interested child into a future needlelacer. And, what is more, into a lacemaker who has been given the right techniques from the start, which is the foundation of all good needlelace.

The author of this book has proved her ability to produce needlelace of a very high standard by winning the 1986 Batsford Prize in the John Bull Trophy awards at the biannual exhibition, which has become a world-wide event held at the English Lace School.

Nenia Lovesey

Introduction

This book is intended to form a complete basic course for the beginner, enabling new lacemakers to work simple pieces of needlepoint lace, and to develop their own ideas and designs. I have given some basic designs to show the complete beginner exactly how to set about working a piece of needlepoint lace for the first time. Each successive design has different threads so that the new lacemaker gains experience in working with a variety of threads.

Once the basics of the technique have been learnt, needlepoint lace lends itself freely and easily to many interpretations and designs, for example, it may be applied to linens and garments, or used for modern, free, three-dimensional lace and for pictures.

Needlepoint lace is a very old form of lacemaking, differing from bobbin lace in using needle and thread to build up the variety of lace stitches. These stitches are based mainly on simple detached buttonhole stitches (blanket stitches) which are worked over a couched thread outline called the cordonnet. Bobbin lace involves the weaving of threads wound on bobbins to build up the lace.

True needlepoint lace developed in the mid-sixteenth century from the earlier cut-work embroidery and reticella, in which some of the warp and weft threads of the fabric were still part of the lace. They formed an open framework over which the lace stitches were worked, giving a geometric look to the lace. The first true needlepoint, *punto in aria* or 'stitch in the air', was worked on a framework of couched threads on parchment. It was independent of the fabric and so could be more free-flowing and curving in design.

These needlepoint laces are thought to have originated principally in Italy, especially Venice, and then spread to other countries, which then developed their own lace industries. The history of lace is a fascinating study in itself for any lacemaker, especially when combined with visits to museums which have lace collections.

one

Equipment

Needlepoint-lace materials are fairly basic and easily obtainable. (A selection of suppliers is listed at the end of the book.) The actual lace stitches are worked with a ball-pointed needle. A variety of threads, preferably smooth for traditional work, may be used. The choice depends on the worker's own preferences and the lace design, always provided that the threads chosen do not 'fluff' or break easily. For basic beginnings and practice, crochet cottons are excellent. Later, finer silk threads, such as 100/3, and fine lace threads produce beautiful effects, as do some metallic and iridescent threads, provided they wash or clean well.

1 *Needlepoint lace equipment.*

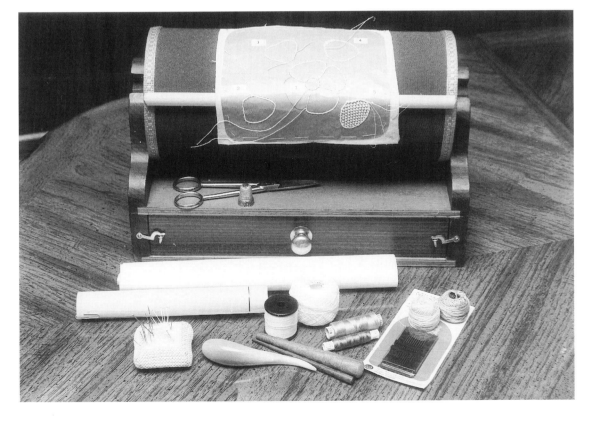

Basic requirements

1 Ball-pointed sewing needles for the lace stitches.
2 Ordinary fine sewing needles for tacking and couching.
3 Pins.
4 Fine-pointed scissors.
5 Thimble.
6 Threads: Each design in this book has details of suitable threads. The first simple daisy motif uses crochet cottons 20 and 40 which are excellent for the beginner. A variety of threads is used in the other designs so that the lacemaker gains experience by working with a range of threads.
7 Ordinary fine sewing cotton, colour-matched with the chosen thread, for couching down the outline cordonnet.
8 15cm square (6in square) of blue or green adhesive plastic or acetate film (similar to that used for covering books) to cover the design and contrast with the threads. Architect's linen may also be used, but is perhaps less easily available.
9 20cm × 40cm (8in × 16in) plain calico for the backing which is later removed and can be used again.
10 Suitable design.
11 Needlepoint lace pillow (optional, but very useful for a good tension).

Making a simple needlepoint lace pillow

A needlepoint lace pillow is of great help in obtaining a good tension and even lace stitches as it leaves both hands free. You can buy one from a lace supplier, but it is quite easy to make your own simple pillow.

Method 1
Find a large tin with a circumference of approximately 40–45cm (16–18in) and a length of approximately 20–25cm (8–10in). Pad the tin with layers of

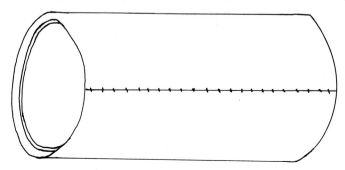

2 Making a pillow from a tin: padding the tin.

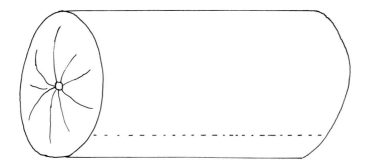

carpet felt or thick material to a depth of about 3–4cm (1–1½in), so that the complete length of a pin can be stuck into the material. Do not cover the ends of the tin with the thick material [2]. Now cover the padded tin with a dark, plain, smooth, natural-fibre fabric, such as cotton, so that it looks like a bolster [3]. The open end (where the lid or top was) can be left open to hold cottons, etc., but make sure there are no sharp edges. Or, if a heavier pillow is preferred, fill the tin with clean, dry sand before putting on the lid and covering.

Method 2

Use part of a roll of polystyrene wall lining. The rolls are usually about 60cm (24in) long, and so one roll would make three cheap light pillows, either to share with friends or to keep as spares. Preferably keeping the roll in its heat-sealed plastic wrap, cut it carefully into three equal pieces [4]. Cover each pillow with a dark, smooth natural fabric, such as cotton, making a bolster shape.

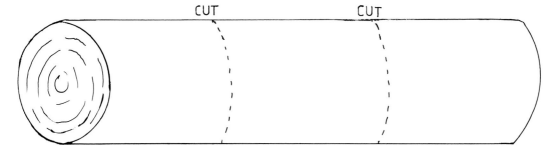

A pillow usually needs a base to stop it rolling. You can use a cushion, or a small plastic box, such as an ice-cream container. Alternatively, you can make a wooden stand, which will keep it in a stable position at a convenient height. I find that the height of the pillow is important, so spend some time deciding where it is most comfortable. For instance, you might prefer to work with the pillow on your lap, or else on a table.

4 Making a pillow from a long polystyrene roll.

Equipment

When you use a pillow, pin the couched work on its calico backing directly onto the pillow, while you work the filling lace stitches and final cordonnette. I find it is helpful to have a stick, such as a piece of dowel 1cm (just under $\frac{1}{2}$in) in diameter or a chopstick, to raise the portion being worked. It is important to pin the work on correctly so that the stick lies along the line of work. When the direction of the stitches is altered, the work must be unpinned and moved, so that the stick once again lies along the line of the stitches [5]. Not everyone uses a pillow, but I have found that when using the traditional English method of working towards you, it produces a nice, even tension to the lace stitches as both hands are left free.

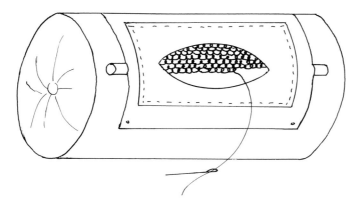

5 *Positioning the work on a pillow.*

two
Stages in working

The five stages of working

The working of a piece of needlelace can be divided into five basic stages:

1 Preparation of the calico backing and the design.
2 Couching the outline threads (called the 'cordonnet').
3 Working the lace stitches in the areas to be filled within the outline.
4 Working stitches over the outline cordonnet (called the 'cordonnette').
5 Removal of the finished lace from the calico backing.

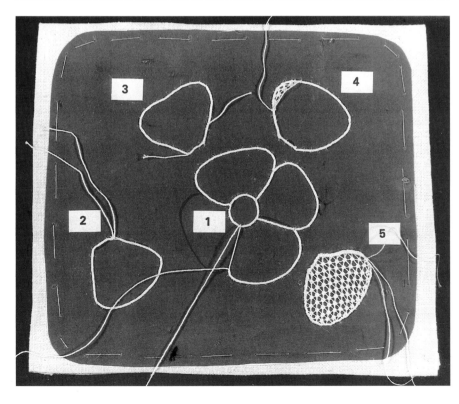

6 Steps in working a piece of needlepoint lace (1. Cordonnet with branches. 2. Interlocking starting loop. 3. Whipping cordonnet ends. 4. Starting lace filling stitches. 5. Buttonholing the cordonnette.)

17

I Preparation and design

Backing

For a small 'beginning design', use a piece of calico 20cm × 40cm (8in × 16in) as the backing. Larger designs require a larger piece, as you need to leave a margin of a least 5cm (2in) around the tacked design particularly if you are using a pillow. However, if the piece is too large it will be awkward.

FOLD

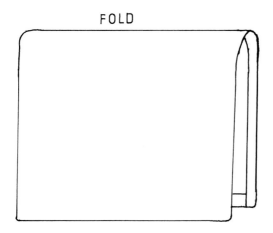

7 *Folding the calico backing.*

FOLD

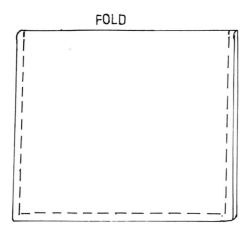

8 *Tacking the folded calico.*

Fold the calico in half, then turn in 1cm ($\frac{3}{8}$in) all round [7] and tack together. (Do not machine as the stitches are pulled out later.) This gives a double thickness backing which is sufficient if a stiffish calico is used [8]. Should the material be softer, then a larger piece can be folded to make three thicknesses before turning in the edges [9].

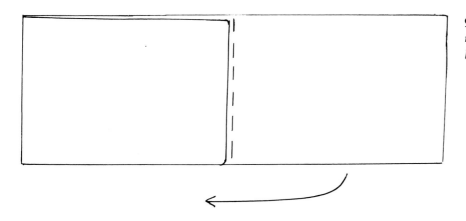

9 *Folding softer material for the backing.*

Design

Trace or draw the chosen design onto plain paper. Most of the beginner's designs in this book have numbers on them to show the start and direction of laying the cordonnet threads. When designing, keep the outlines simple and clear. Avoid long thin designs, unless they are to be applied to a fabric, as the lace will tend to twist and go out of shape if free. Most lacemakers enjoy making up their own designs as needlepoint lace is very adaptable.

Use a piece of blue or green adhesive acetate film which is sufficiently large to cover the design and leave at least 3cm (1¼in) clear around the outline. Peel off the backing and lay the film over the design. (I also round off the corners to prevent any threads catching on them later.) This covering prevents the needle from catching and tearing the design when working since the actual lace stitches are all worked on the surface of the design.

The colour of the acetate film is important as it should contrast with the colour of the threads used in the lace. For most work, blue or green is generally used, but if the lace is worked in blue or green, then obviously a clear or yellow acetate makes a better contrast. (It is worthwhile mentioning here that very dark colour threads are more difficult to see when working than paler colours.) Should the shine on the film distract you, then gently buff over the surface with wire wool.

If you are unable to obtain a certain colour film, then draw the design onto coloured paper and use a clear acetate film, such as is used to cover books.

Architect's linen can also be used to cover the design with the matt surface uppermost, or the design can be drawn onto the shiny back surface, but remember it will then be in reverse.

Tack the design (under its film) around the edge onto the prepared calico backing, making sure any knots are underneath as they will otherwise catch annoyingly as you work [10].

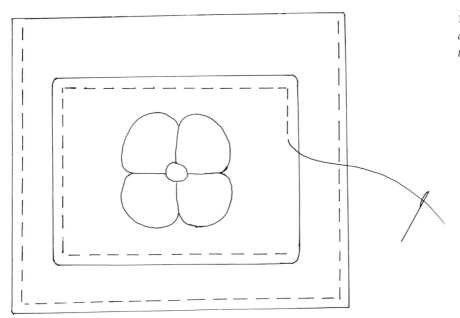

You are now ready to start the actual lace by couching down the cordonnet outline threads.

2 Couching the cordonnet outline

The outline threads of the lace are called the cordonnet. They form the framework for the lace, within which the lace stitches are worked. It is, therefore, very important that as much care and attention are given to the cordonnet as to the lace stitches, since a poor framework will obviously result in a disappointing piece of lace.

In the detailed instructions for many of the designs in this book a suitable start and the direction of couching down the cordonnet are shown by numbers. In these numbered designs you will commence at 1 and work along the outline following the numbers. If you are right-handed it is best to work towards the left so that your left hand holds the outline threads in position as you couch them down, turning the work about as necessary. If you are left-handed it is best to work towards the right.

Ideally, you should try to lay the cordonnet threads along the whole design outline without any breaks. It is important, therefore, to think carefully before you start any piece of lace. The cordonnet is laid as a double thread which is couched down along its length through all the layers of calico backing, design and acetate film. The cordonnet thread is usually

20

slightly thicker than that used for the lace stitches, but where a particularly fine edge is required I use the same thread.

The first step is to estimate how much thread is needed to go continuously (if possible) along all the outlines. You can do this by actually laying the thread, still running from the spool or ball, along the outlines as an estimate. In the first basic daisy motif this will be the Number 20 crochet cotton. Add a little extra to compensate for errors and allow for finishing, then double this length and fold it in half. Cut off, but do *not* cut the looped end as this is used to begin your cordonnet. Later the cordonnet will also 'lock' into this starting loop.

Using a normal length of a matching or sympathetic thin sewing cotton and an ordinary fine sewing needle, make a knot or double backstitch on the back of the calico foundation under the number 1 on the design, or under the starting point of any other design. Bring your needle up through all the layers to the upper side exactly at 1 so that you are ready with your cotton to couch down the cordonnet threads from this point.

Begin the couching by making the first couching stitch hold down the looped end of the cordonnet thread [11]. Keeping the two cordonnet threads parallel and fairly taut so that they do not pucker, couch them down, going right through all the layers and making your stitches about 3mm ($\frac{1}{8}$in) apart.

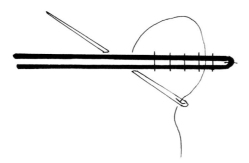

11 *Commencing the couching down of the cordonnet. In the actual lace the cordonnet threads lie closely* side by side.

The stitch should be just long enough to hold the two threads touching side by side. It is also advisable to check the back to make sure you do not leave slackness or loops in the couching cotton.

If you were couching the cordonnet for a simple circle, you would continue all around the outline until you reached the starting loop. Whatever your design, it is essential to interlock this starting loop into your cordonnet, so that the lace does not fall apart later. To do this, pass the two cordonnet threads, but not the couching cotton, through the starting loop. In a simple circle design you would then be ready to end off your cordonnet, so lay one of the cordonnet threads back along your just-couched cordonnet and whip this firmly and closely to the cordonnet for approximately 2cm ($\frac{3}{4}$in), keeping on the surface of the acetate film and not going

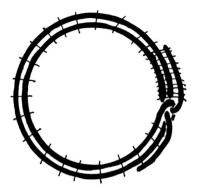

12 *End the cordonnet threads by passing through the starting loop and whipping down on the surface.*

through any of the layers [12]. Whip the other cordonnet thread down in the same manner, but in the opposite direction. Now take your couching cotton straight down through the layers and fasten off at the back. Cut off the cordonnet threads closely [13].

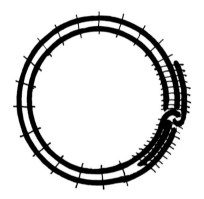

13 *Cut off the whipped cordonnet threads.*

In a more elaborate design, such as the daisy motif in Chapter 3, you would obviously not be ending off at this point. Instead, you would interlock the starting loop by passing the two cordonnet threads through it as previously explained (a fine crochet hook is useful for this), and continue the couching along the design outline. In the daisy motif, this would be to number 5 and then around to number 6.

Where there are branches off in a design, for example at 6 in the daisy motif, you only take one of the cordonnet threads down and back, so giving a double thread again, interlocking your cordonnet by passing this thread under the already couched cordonnet at the point of meeting. Again a fine crochet hook is useful here. If both cordonnet threads were taken down and back the resulting four threads would be too thick in comparison with the rest of the work. Always take the correct thread down in a design so that the cordonnet threads do not cross [14]. You then continue the cordonnet along

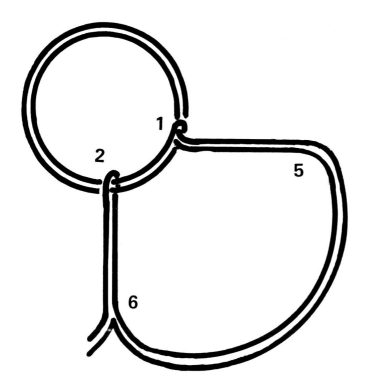

14 Working a branch in the cordonnet.

the outlines of the design as usual, making similar branches where necessary.

The cordonnet is generally best worked from the inner part of the design outwards so that the threads have somewhere to interlock where necessary. Interlocking is essential in order to give a stable framework to the lace. If you find that the end of the branch does not touch an already couched part of the cordonnet, you must remember to interlock the end when you do pass it during further couching down. If, by some chance, you forget to interlock at a junction, then you may be able to remedy it when working your lace filling stitches, by making a lace stitch hold the abutting cordonnet threads. However, this is an emergency measure only!

When you reach the end, your cordonnet threads must be whipped securely, as mentioned earlier, by taking both under the existing couched cordonnet near by and whipping them down in opposite directions.

Where there is an elaborate design you may need to bring in new branches of the cordonnet from one part of the design to another. This can be done by passing a single new cordonnet thread under and out over the existing couched cordonnet at the required point, thus giving a double cordonnet thread ready to couch down, avoiding more starting loops [15].

There is an alternative method of laying the cordonnet. In this method,

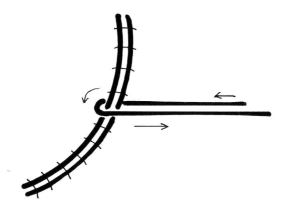

15 *Bringing a new thread into an already couched cordonnet of an elaborate design.*

the small couching threads are put in first around the outline and then the cordonnet threads are threaded through them to form the outline cordonnet.

If you run out of cordonnet thread, you may butt the end of one thread, making sure it is not near a similar join [16], but try to avoid this.

16 *Butting the ends.*

3 Working the lace filling stitches

The basic needlepoint lace stitch is the blanket, or simple detached buttonhole stitch [17]. Variety of stitch is mainly achieved by altering the

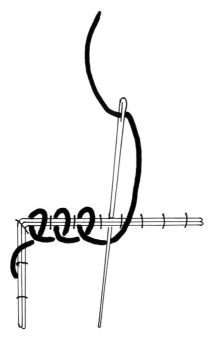

17 *The basic needlepoint lace stitch worked over the two couched cordonnet threads.*

24

number and arrangement of these stitches. More stitches are shown in Chapter 4, and you can extend your repertoire still further by studying other needlepoint lace books.

The beauty of lace lies not only in its texture and design, but also in the tension and evenness of the stitches. It is, therefore, advisable to make a practice sampler to try out stitches. A sampler can also be used to see whether different types and thicknesses of thread suit a particular stitch. (See Chapter 6.)

Making a sampler

To make a sampler 20cm × 30cm (8in × 12in), use a piece of calico for the base approximately 50cm × 35cm (20in × 14in). Tack a single 1.5cm ($\frac{5}{8}$in) hem all round. Fold the calico in half and catch-stitch or machine around the edge.

You will then require 2.5m (just over 2½yd) of flat tape 1cm ($\frac{3}{8}$in) wide to make up the sampler areas. Leaving approximately 4cm (1½in) clear at the top and lower edges of the calico base and 2cm ($\frac{3}{4}$in) at the sides, draw grid lines with tailor's chalk or pencil [18] to form 16 'boxes'.

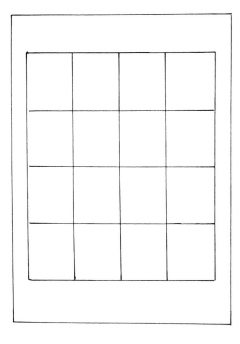

18 *Mark out the position of the tapes.*

continued overleaf

Position the centre of your tape over the grid lines, and tack and machine (or backstitch) along these lines [19]. Machine down the centre of the tape, so that the edges are left free. It is advisable to stitch the outside tape last as it will hold the end of the tapes in place.

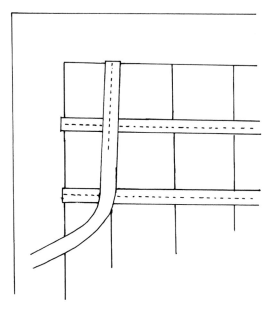

19 *Stitch down the centre of the tapes.*

This will give you 16 sample areas. Should you wish to make a sampler with more spaces, increase the dimensions of the calico base and tape length accordingly. You may also prefer to use a coloured cotton material for the base to show up the stitches. In Chapter 4 the sampler idea is developed into a cushion.

Having made a sampler or couched down the cordonnet of a design, lace filling stitches are then worked with a ball-pointed needle completely on the surface; they do not go through any of the layers. The ball-pointed needle (such as is used for sewing jersey-type fabrics) prevents the needle from piercing the surface, or splitting the thread when working. It is advisable to use the smallest available size which can be comfortably threaded with your chosen thread. A Number 40 crochet cotton is ideal for initial practice with your sampler. The first 'daisy' motif in Chapter 3 also uses this thread.

Starting and ending-off

Using a ball-pointed sewing needle threaded with a length – not more than 50cm (20in) – of Number 40 crochet cotton or other chosen thread, fasten on firmly by running the thread under three or four of the cordonnet couching stitches near the point where you wish to begin. Work two inward-facing blanket or detached buttonhole stitches firmly at this point. You are then ready to work your lace filling stitches [20].

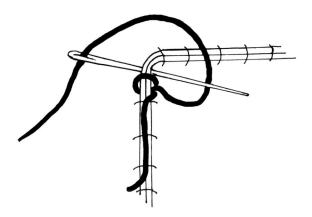

20 *Fastening on the working thread.*

When you run out of thread or need to end off, you can just reverse the process. Work two firm outward-facing buttonhole stitches and run the thread under three or four of the couching stitches before cutting it off. **To avoid 'lumpiness' I run the starting and ending-off threads under the couching in opposite directions. Remember, start again at the side where you ended off!**

There are other ways of starting and ending, one of which is mentioned in the instructions for working the first petal of the daisy motif in Chapter 3. When you are practising on a sampler you can obviously start off with a knot or backstitches on the reverse of your sampler.

Single Bruxelles (Brussels) or net stitch

This is the simplest needlepoint lace stitch, but it has a tendency to 'ride up', so making it less easy than it looks! Work a few rows just to get the idea of the basic stitch, then I suggest going on to the corded single Bruxelles, which is a good beginner's stitch as it is much firmer and altogether a more satisfactory stitch to work, especially when you are just starting to learn needlepoint lace.

Fasten on at the left-hand side of your sampler square about 3mm ($\frac{1}{8}$in) from the top. If you are left-handed you might prefer to begin at the right, but you do have to work in both directions in any case. The first row in the sampler square uses the top tape instead of a couched cordonnet, as in an ordinary piece of lace. Take a stitch downwards into the top tape below the machine stitches, about 3mm ($\frac{1}{8}$in) along from the left-hand edge, and bring the needle through and out so that it catches the loop left by the thread. Gently pull up the stitch slightly, so making your first single Bruxelles stitch.

Leaving about 3mm ($\frac{1}{8}$in) between the stitches, work to the end of the row. This spacing is only a suggestion for practising the basic net stitch, as it can be worked closer or further apart to vary the effect. Do not pull the stitches too tightly. At the end of the row take the thread under and out through the right-hand side tape [21b].

21a *Single Bruxelles or net stitch.*

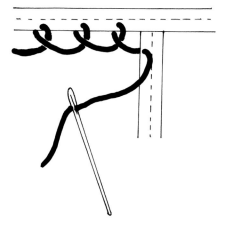

21b *Single Bruxelles stitch: at the end of the first row of the sampler square.*

To be at the right depth for the row back, whip under and over the tape slightly lower down, then work your row from right to left taking a stitch into each loop between the stitches of the row above. If you find difficulty in working the rows from right to left, then 'throw' the thread down and across to the left before taking the needle down through the loop of the stitch above [22].

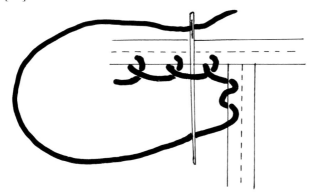

22 *Single Bruxelles stitch: working across to the left.*

At the end of the row, again take the thread under and out through the side tape. Now whip once to be at the right depth to start the next row, working from left to right again. When you are working in a regular shape or sampler square you need to keep the number of stitches constant, so if you use the first loop in a row do not work the last, or if you do not go into the first loop, then you will use the last loop.

This stitch has a tendency to 'ride' up, making it difficult to achieve an even tension. If you are working on a pillow, you can put in one or two pins to hold the rows down in place. If you are working a large area, or are not using a pillow, then you can hold the stitches down in place by joining in a tacking thread every few rows. Whip it over and under the loops across the row to the other side [23]. Pull up firmly so that the row is in position in a

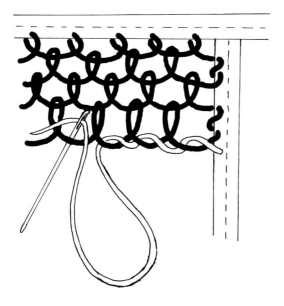

23 *Single Bruxelles stitch: holding down rows by whipping with a tacking thread.*

29

straight line and end off the holding thread. (This very useful method was shown to me by Carol Williamson.) When you work the next row after putting in a holding thread, just ignore it and work as if it was not there. These threads are removed when the area is completed.

When your area of net stitch is completed, you finish by whipping down the loops of the last row to the tape or cordonnet, still with the thread you have been using [24]. I find it gives a better tension if you have to pull the lace down very slightly to do this, but not too much. Also whipping into every loop in this stitch achieves a better effect than leaving some out, or even working the last row into the tape as this seems to give an unwanted ridge.

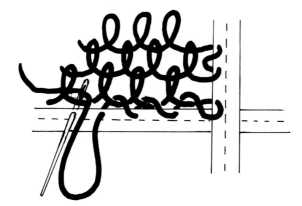

24 *Single Bruxelles stitch: whipping last row to the tape.*

Corded single Bruxelles – sometimes called linen or corded stitch

This is one of my favourite stitches as it works up with a good even tension and gives depth to a design, contrasting well with more open lacier stitches [25]. In fact, this is the first stitch I always teach to beginners since it is

25 *Corded single Bruxelles or corded stitch, with a four-hole diamond and a row of twisted single Bruxelles.*

satisfactory to work, producing a rhythmic feeling to the work which results in a good tension.

Fasten on as before in another sampler square. If you are right-handed it is best to work the stitches from left to right. Work a row of the single detached buttonhole stitches into the top tape (or cordonnet in a design), so that they do not quite touch each other. They can be worked very closely, but it is easier for the beginner to have the stitches fractionally apart. At the end of the row, simply take the needle under and up out through the right-hand tape (or left, if you are left-handed and wish to work in the opposite direction).

Bring your thread immediately back across to the other side and take the needle under and out through the tape this side, so laying the 'cord' which gives the stitch its name. The thread of this cord should lie just below the loops of the stitches in the row above [26].

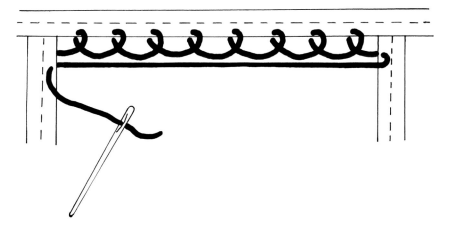

26 Corded single Bruxelles stitch: laying the cord.

To get yourself to the right depth for the next row of stitches, pass the needle under and up through the tape again fractionally lower, so that you are a stitch depth below the first row of stitches.

27 *Corded single Bruxelles stitch: needle behind loop and cord.*

Now work your next row of stitches into the loops of the row above, taking in the cord just laid. Your needle, therefore, will pass behind the two threads when working each stitch [27].

Continue working your area, alternately working a row of stitches and laying a cord. If you run out of thread, make sure that you start again at the same side you ended off, otherwise the stitches will slant in a different direction and look odd. When you whip down at the end, do not lay a cord, just whip each loop to the bottom tape and end off.

Whipped single Bruxelles stitch

This is a variation of the basic single Bruxelles or net stitch which is very effective, firmer to work and holds its shape nicely.

Fasten on at the left of another sampler square and work a row of single detached buttonhole stitches, using the top tape as before, and keeping the spacing about 3mm ($\frac{1}{8}$in) apart. As usual, at the end of the row take the needle under and up through the right hand tape. In a piece of lace you would go under the cordonnet.

Now whip back across to the left by taking the needle downwards once through each loop between the stitches, including the first and last loops

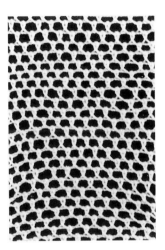

28 *Whipped single Bruxelles stitch.*

[29]. At the end of this whipping row take the needle under and out through the left tape. I think it makes the ends of the rows look better if you come out at the same point as the start of the first buttonhole stitch of the row you have been whipping. If necessary, pull up the thread gently so that it lies more or less straight. To be in position for the next row, whip once under and over the edge of the left tape.

In this next and every successive stitch row work the stitches as usual but take your needle behind the whipped loop so passing behind two threads.

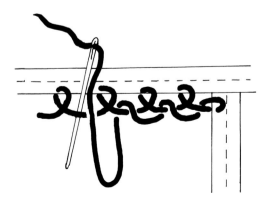

29 *Whipped single Bruxelles stitch: whipping into each loop.*

33

These two rows are repeated until the area is filled. Complete by whipping the last row down to the bottom tape as usual. Do this directly after the row of stitches as you do not need the row of whipping first.

Double Bruxelles stitch

In this stitch, the detached buttonhole stitches are worked in pairs with an equal length gap between each pair group [30].

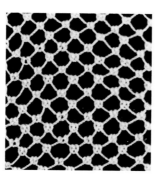

30 *Double Bruxelles stitch.*

Fasten on at the left and work two simple buttonhole stitches, using the top tape as before and placing them so that they just touch. Leave a gap equal to the distance occupied by the last two stitches, then work the next pair of stitches. Work in this way across the row. At the end take the thread under and out through the right tape. If necessary, whip once over the edge of the tape so that you are at the correct depth for the next row.

Work across this and all the rows by taking two stitches into each long loop between the pairs in the previous row [31]. **Keep the thread straight in the gap when working the pairs of stitches, and do not let it loop down, since the pair of stitches worked into it in the next row tends to pull it down anyway.**

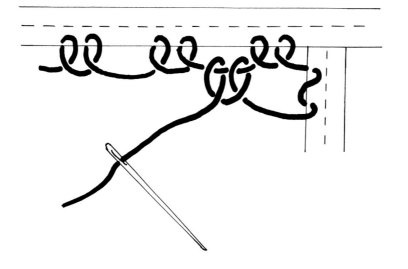

31 *Double Bruxelles stitch: two stitches into each long loop.*

34

As you work this stitch you will notice that the pairs of stitches lie in a diagonal pattern. The beauty of this stitch lies in its regularity, so keep an eye on this diagonal pattern, as well as the stitches in each row, by making sure that the 'holes' are always of equal size.

When the filling is completed, finish by whipping it down to the bottom tape. I prefer to take two whipping down stitches into each long loop so that the pattern is kept here as well [32].

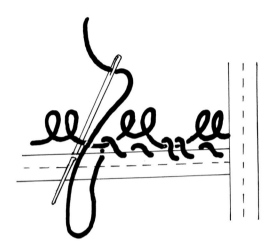

32 *Double Bruxelles stitch: whipping last row to the tape.*

Treble Bruxelles stitch

This is worked in the same manner as the double Bruxelles stitch, except that you work a group of three stitches and leave a space equal to the width of three stitches [33]. It is mainly useful for large areas, or for modern work.

At its completion, keep the pattern by making three whipping stitches when fastening each long loop to the bottom tape.

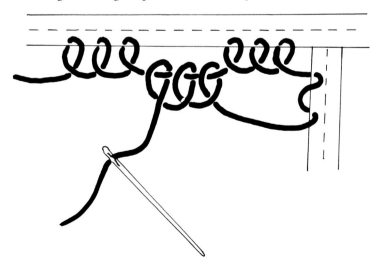

33 *Treble Bruxelles stitch: three stitches into each long loop.*

35

'Lattice-type' corded double Bruxelles filling

This very pretty stitch is almost like an 'opened-out' corded double
Bruxelles stitch [34]. It can also be worked in trebles. The beauty lies in its
regularity, so again keep an eye on the diagonals.

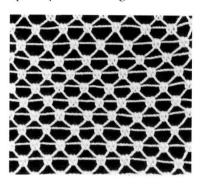

34 *'Lattice-type'
filling stitch.*

Fasten on at the left near the top and work two detached buttonhole
stitches quite closely together, using the top tape of the sampler square as
usual. Leave a space of equal width to the two stitches before making the
next pair, keeping the loop fairly slack so that it will dip down to almost
twice the depth of the stitches. Work in this way to the end of the row, again
ending with a group of two stitches before taking the thread under and out
through the right tape.

Whip once over the edge of the tape, so that you come out and lay a cord
across to the left which will lie just touching the loops of the row above.
Come out through the left tape as usual [35].

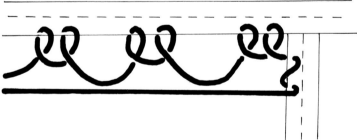

35 *'Lattice-type'
filling stitch: laying
the cord.*

Whip down the tape once or twice so that you are two stitches' depth
down. Work across in pairs of stitches as in the first row. Leaving the loop
fairly slack between each pair group, take the two stitches into each slack
loop above and include the cord, so that the needle passes behind two threads
(as in the corded or linen stitch). **If you are working on a pillow you can
put a pin into each slack loop to hold it down in position. However, I
find that if you pull the loop down gently with the needle point after
making the pair of stitches, it will lie perfectly.**

36

At the end of this row, take the thread under and out through the tape at the same level as the start of this row. Lay the cord straight across to the left, coming up through the tape at the same point as the start of the previous row of stitches.

You will notice that there is a sort of triangular pattern at the ends. Work the pairs of stitches across the row, starting with two stitches into this first part-loop and its cord, and end with the same at the other end. As in the first row, whip over the tape once or twice to the correct depth and lay the cord. Continue working the rows in this manner [36].

You will also notice that alternate rows have one fewer group of doubles. This keeps the correct number of stitches when working a regular area, as in a sampler square.

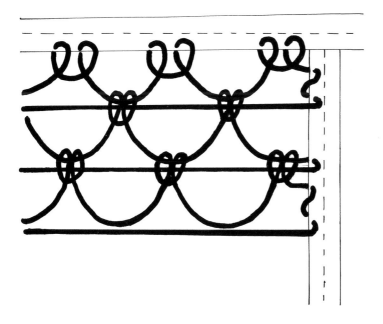

36 *'Lattice-type' filling stitch: pattern at the end of rows.*

On completion, whip the loops down to the bottom tape (as in the double Bruxelles stitch) after working the last row of stitches.

This stitch has been given in some detail so that you get used to looking at the 'ends' of rows and keeping them in the correct pattern. This will be helpful when thinking about the row ends in an uneven shape, as in most pieces of lace. Probably by now, you will find also that you can almost work from a photograph or diagram of lace without needing too many instructions. These lace stitches should have given you a good idea of working needlepoint lace fillings; others are given in Chapter 4. Either try a few of these as well or go on to the first simple motif.

Increasing and decreasing

When you need to increase, you work the extra number of stitches into the cordonnet at the necessary end of the row, at either the beginning or the end, still keeping the pattern correct. You also decrease at the ends of the rows by leaving out the required number of stitches. (See also Chapter 3.)

4 Buttonholing the cordonnette

Most laces are completed with a buttonholed edging around the motif or *toilé* called the cordonnette. This cordonnette can be simple, or more padded and elaborate as in some of the Venetian raised laces. (See Chapter 5.)

When you are working the cordonnette on a motif, obviously all the lace filling stitches must have been completed before you start. The cordonnette gives a 'finish' to a piece of lace. It also covers up any unevenness and ends since it is worked over the cordonnet.

However, when I work such things as tiny three-dimensional flowers in cloth stitch, I often prefer not to work any cordonnette, so as to keep them more naturalistic. In this way, they often curl attractively as well, but you do have to be fanatically neat when working the lace filling stitches.

The cordonnette on the least important parts of a padded or large motif is often worked first, so that the important areas are made to stand out more obviously. To achieve this, you will find you generally begin near the outside and work inwards, whereas in laying your original cordonnet outline it is usually the opposite.

The buttonhole stitches of the cordonnette and the threads laid under the stitches are generally worked in the same thread as used for the lace filling stitches, unless a padded outline is desired. (See Chapter 5.) In most laces the stitches are worked over two (or sometimes more) threads which are laid immediately over the cordonnet, but are not couched down first. More details are given in the instructions for the daisy motif in Chapter 3 and in Chapter 5 which deals with padded outlines.

Starting

First, decide where you are going to start off the cordonnette; it is usually best to start at a junction in your outline. Fasten on your working thread in the usual way at this point, just as you would when working lace filling stitches. As you generally work over two laid threads, make them from a long one doubled over so that you have a loop. This will enable you to secure it when you begin your buttonholing. Bring your needle up through this loop and then work your buttonhole stitches. If possible, the laid threads should be long enough to go continuously around the outlines of the whole design if it is not too complex.

The two laid threads lie exactly over the cordonnet. The buttonhole stitches are worked so that the needle passes under the cordonnet each time, which means that every stitch includes the cordonnet edge as well as the laid

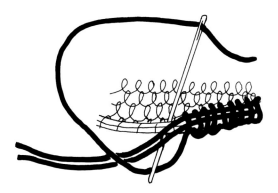

37 *The cordonnette: the needle passes under the cordonnet when making each cordonnette buttonhole stitch.*

threads [37]. Remember, all your work is still on the surface; the needle does not pass through into the design and foundation.

You usually work the buttonhole stitches with the 'loops' of each stitch towards the outside. I find it best to work towards yourself, stitching from right to left if you are right-handed. This is helpful because the left-hand thumb can hold the laid threads in place as you work. If your work is pinned to a needlepoint pillow it leaves both hands free, thus producing an even tension to the stitches. As you work the cordonnette, check occasionally to make sure that it always encloses the cordonnet outline threads, ensuring that the back of the work is also neat.

Joins
Should you run out of one of the laid threads when working your cordonnette, simply butt the ends as you would when laying the outline cordonnet.

You can end off and start a new working thread as you would when working lace filling stitches. If you make the two fastening buttonhole stitches lie under the threads that are being laid down for your cordonnette, they will be covered, thus ensuring a smooth edge.

Branches
Take one of the threads down and back along the branch, as you would when laying the outline cordonnet. It is obviously not couched, but the end

is held by taking it under and over the cordonnet [38]. Further details are given in the instructions for the cordonnette of the first simple daisy motif in the next chapter.

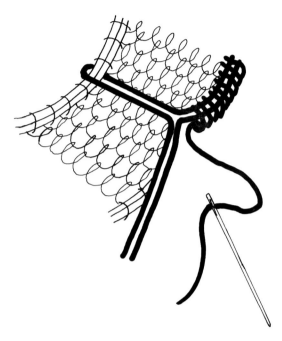

38 *Branches in the cordonnette laid threads.*

Ending off
When the cordonnette has been completed, you just cut off the two laid threads closely. To cover any ends which may possibly be showing, you can

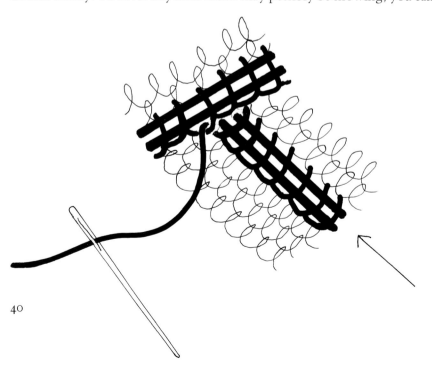

39 *Ending off the cordonnette.*

then work another simple buttonhole stitch over the outline. Before ending your working thread, link this last stitch to the most immediate loop of the nearby cordonnette stitches by taking the needle through this loop [39]. Make one or two tight ending-off detached buttonhole stitches, run the thread under the cordonnette stitches a short way and cut it off closely.

5 Removing the finished lace

This is probably the most exciting stage. Remove the tacking stitches from the edges of the calico foundation, and also those which held the covered design edges to it.

The lace is now only held onto the design and foundation by the outline cordonnet couching. Never try to cut the lace off from the surface. Part the two layers of the calico backing. Then, using sharp pointed scissors, snip the couching threads which lie between them, thus freeing your lace.

Rather than lifting the lace straight off the covered design, I prefer to lift the acetate-covered design with the lace, pulling out any visible couching threads, and then to gently remove the lace from the acetate. This avoids any possible distortion of your lace by pulling. The upper side facing you when you made your lace is the right side of the lace.

Finally, you just need to pull out any ends of the couching stitches from the underside of your lace. Tweezers are very useful for this.

three

Making a simple motif

Useful hints

1 The adhesive acetate film over your design should be in a contrasting colour to your thread, so that you can see the stitches clearly. Blue or green is restful on the eyes.

2 **Spend time on the couching of the cordonnet, since it is the framework of your lace.**

3 Try to get into a rhythm as you work your lace stitches, watching each stitch and loop as you make them. This helps both your tension and evenness.

4 Do not stop in the middle of a row when working. If possible work a whole area before stopping.

5 Watch the end of the rows. Keep them level and avoid unwanted gaps between the stitches and the cordonnet.

6 Do not pull the stitches too tightly; the beauty of the lace fillings is in the appearance of each stitch as well as the pattern.

7 Avoid letting the thread twist up too much. It helps if the needle is threaded with the free end of the thread on the spool.

8 You can not really join on in the middle of a row. You need a length of thread at least three or four times the width of the row to get across easily.

9 When you join on a new thread while working the lace fillings, make sure that you are beginning at the side where you have just ended off.

10 If the couching stitches of the cordonnet get in the way when working the fillings, take the needle through them diagonally. Actually, they are often useful to hold your rows in position.

11 When you are at the end of a row, remember the thread should then pass under the cordonnet at that side so that the next row starts with the thread lying over the cordonnet [40].

12 If you need to undo stitches, take them out one at a time with the needle point, holding down the stitch behind with the thumbnail of your other hand. This prevents everything from tightening up.

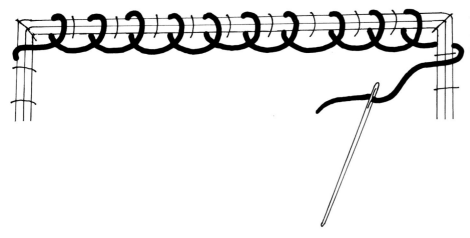

40 *Thread under the cordonnet at the end of a row.*

A basic four-petalled stylized flower shape, here called the daisy motif, has been chosen as it will take you through all the stages of working a simple piece of needlepoint lace [41]. Instructions for working this basic shape are given in detail, together with diagrams (refer back to Chapter 2 if necessary). In addition, two alternative methods are given to enable you to adapt and develop a basic shape.

The original piece was worked in white mercerized crochet cotton Number 40 and put onto a black velvet-type backing under a paperweight. A cream or écru motif would look well on a brown background. Obviously almost any colour thread can be chosen depending on personal preference, but remember that paler colours are the easiest to work with.

Daisy motif

Materials
- Number 20 crochet cotton for the cordonnet in the same colour as the Number 40.
- Number 40 crochet cotton for the lace stitches
- Matching sewing cotton for the couching
- Calico foundation backing
- Acetate film

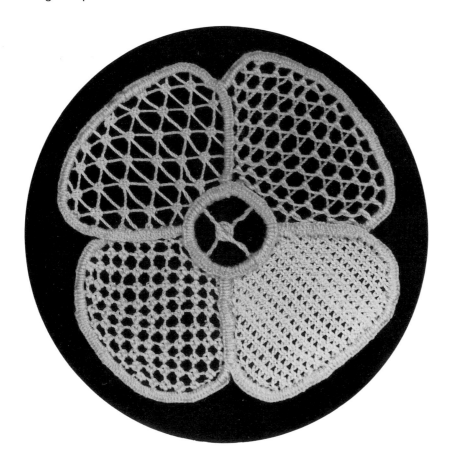

41 *Worked basic daisy motif (enlarged).*

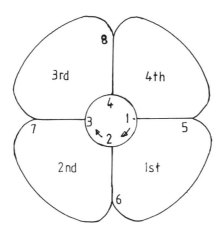

42 *Daisy motif.*

Preparation

Draw or trace the daisy motif [42] onto a small sheet of plain white drawing paper. Place it under a piece of blue or green adhesive acetate film, or pale blue architect's linen, and trim off the excess so that you are left with a square, which has a 3cm ($1\frac{1}{4}$in) border around the design outline. You can round off the corners slightly, so that threads do not catch on them. Tack the design under its film onto a prepared calico backing, which should allow for a clear 5cm (2in) around the tacked design. This can be less if you do not use a pillow. Keep any knots on the underside. You are now ready to couch the cordonnet.

The cordonnet

Estimate the length of Number 20 crochet cotton required to go continuously along the design lines by first placing the single thread along them. Allowing a little extra, double the measurement and then fold this length over and cut it off from the ball. Do not cut the looped end. In this way you now have a double thread to go along the design lines and form the cordonnet. In this motif you will find you need approximately 100cm (40in) of thread doubled over to give a double cordonnet thread of 50cm (20in) length. This method can be used with almost any design to estimate the amount required for the cordonnet.

Using a single strand of thin matching sewing cotton and an ordinary fairly fine sewing needle, make a knot or double backstitch on the underside of the calico immediately under the number 1. Bring the sewing cotton up onto the surface exactly at 1 so that you are ready to couch down the cordonnet from this point, remembering that the first stitch will hold the looped end of your cordonnet. (See Chapter 2.) A thimble is of great help in the couching, even if you do not normally wear one, as it will save holes in your fingers.

Couch the two cordonnet threads down exactly side by side around the centre circle, passing numbers 2, 3 and 4 and making your stitches about 3mm ($\frac{1}{8}$in) apart. When almost back to 1 remember to pass the two cordonnet threads (but not the couching cotton) through the starting loop to interlock it.

Continue the couching down the side of the first petal, passing 5 and going round to 6, where there is a branch in the outline. Take the inner thread only down to 2, and pass it under the couched cordonnet circle at 2 (a fine crochet hook is of use here). Bring the now-interlocked thread back to 6, so achieving a double thread to the cordonnet [6]. Couch this double thread down.

The two cordonnet threads should always lie parallel and just touching.

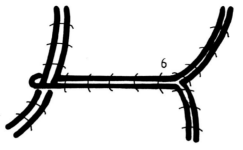

For neatness and firmness at a branch (as at 6), make the couching hold the cordonnet threads exactly in position, so that there is no little triangular gap left when this inner thread again rejoins the other [43].

Continue couching down the cordonnet, making similar branches at 7 and 8. When you are back at 5 you will need to end off the cordonnet. Pass both cordonnet threads under the previously couched cordonnet at 5, then lay one thread back towards 8. Still using the couching cotton, whip this thread down quite closely to the couched cordonnet for at least 1cm ($\frac{1}{2}$in), keeping on the surface and not going down into the acetate film. Lay the other thread in the opposite direction towards 6 and whip this one down in the same way. Take your couching cotton straight through to the underside, fasten off on the back of the calico and cut it off. Cut off the ends of the cordonnet threads quite closely to the whipping.

Working the lace filling stitches

The right side of your work is the upper surface which is facing you. The lace filling stitches in this motif are worked so that the rows run sideways [44] rather than horizontally across the petal. This is in order to avoid unnecessarily awkward shapes for anyone beginning needlepoint lace for the first time. If you worked horizontally across the petal there would be a

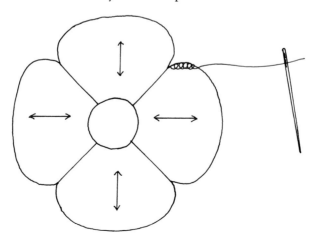

44 *Direction of working lace filling stitches.*

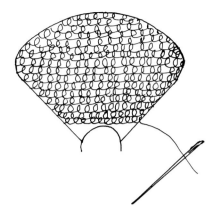

difficult shape at the base of each petal [45]. Obviously, when more experienced, the lacemaker will often work the stitches in a motif to follow and emphasize the flowing line and curve of a design. Indeed, part of the interest and beauty of a needlepoint lace design is in working the stitches to bring out and emphasize the movement in a design. Refer back to your sampler and the instructions in Chapter 2 if necessary, when working the four types of stitch used in this motif.

First petal
The first petal is worked in corded single Bruxelles stitch (sometimes also called corded stitch). This is a firm stitch, which gives depth to a design, as well as a contrasting area for the more open lace stitches.

The rows will be worked parallel to an imaginary line drawn down the centre of the petal. If you wish, you can actually make a guiding line at the centre on the acetate film. Press gently but firmly with the point of your ball-point needle until it leaves an impression, which will give you a guide in keeping the rows straight.

Using the ball-pointed needle threaded with a length of Number 40 crochet cotton – about 50cm (20in) is adequate – fasten on at 5 just below the branching of the cordonnet at the side of the petal [46]. You can fasten on by

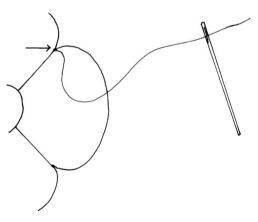

46 Fastening on near cordonnet branch (right-handed).

47

running the thread under three or four of the couching stitches below and then working two inward facing buttonhole stitches at the point where you wish to start. Another way, which is especially useful for fine threads, is to make an immediate inward facing buttonhole stitch with an extra twist to it (almost like a French knot), then another ordinary buttonhole close to it. Pull up tightly and give a little tug to the thread to make sure it is firm, then cut off the tail-end quite closely. (Shown to me by Carol Williamson.)

In needlepoint lace you usually work stitches in both directions, but it is often easier for a right-handed worker to work from left to right, and vice versa if you are left-handed. Therefore, anyone left-handed might find it more convenient to fasten on at the other side [47] and work in the reverse direction to the instructions.

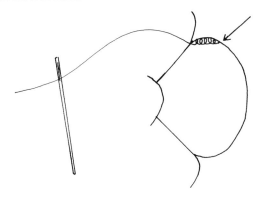

47 Fastening on and working first row (left-handed).

Work your first row of stitches across to the other side, making them lie so that they do not quite touch each other. At the end of the row, take the thread under the cordonnet. You should have a row which is parallel to your centre indentation.

Now lay the cord across to the left, by taking your needle under the cordonnet on the left, so that the thread lies just below the loops of the stitches above. If you find the thread does not lie flat, you can make an inward-facing buttonhole on the right before laying the cord [48]. **In order to make sure that you take your cord across to the right point, you can place it in position with your hand first and then take the needle under the cordonnet where the thread touches it.**

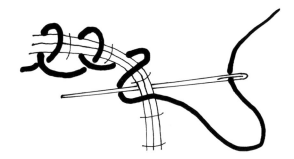

48 Petal one: inward facing buttonhole stitch before laying the cord if necessary to hold it in place.

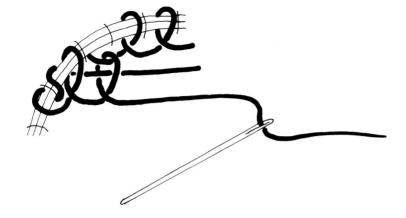

The shape of the petal here will require you to increase at the start of this, and some of the other rows. To do this, simply whip once down the cordonnet to be at the right depth for the next row, then work your first stitch into the cordonnet [49] before working across this row. Now, work across the row, remembering that your needle will be passing behind the loop of the stitch above and also behind the cord as you work each stitch. At the end of the row you can increase similarly by working your extra stitch into the right hand cordonnet. Complete the row by passing the thread under this cordonnet, before laying your cord.

Continue your corded single Bruxelles filling of the first petal, making sure that the rows are straight by keeping the ends level. When you need to decrease, you just omit the stitch at the required end of the row. Should you find this leaves a gap you can whip this stitch down after laying the cord [50].

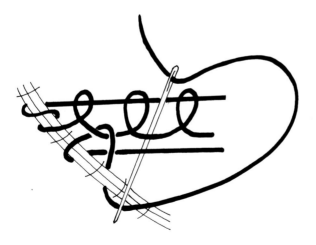

50 *Avoiding a gap when decreasing at the start of a row.*

When your filling stitches for the petal are complete, do not lay a cord. Instead, whip the last row down to the cordonnet with your working thread, just as with the sampler, taking a whip stitch into each loop [51].

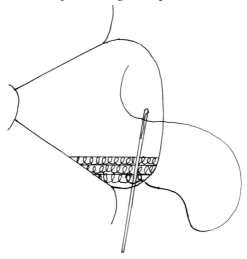

Should you still have a long length of working thread left, there is no need to cut it off here since the lace stitches of the second petal can be worked with it. Simply whip under and over the cordonnet once or twice until you are at the correct starting point for the second petal.

Second petal
This is worked in double Bruxelles stitch. It is next to the petal you have just worked and so the cordonnet between the two is shared, without disturbing the stitches. Just ignore the corded single Bruxelles (corded stitch) on the other side of it.

You commence the lace filling stitches for this second petal (and the other petals) at a similar point to petal one. If you wish, again mark the centre guiding line of your petal on the acetate as before. You will also need to turn your work as you begin each new petal.

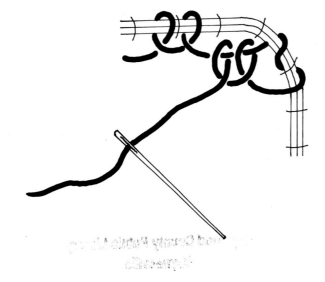

52 *Petal two: double Bruxelles stitch.*

Work the first row of double Bruxelles stitches (see Chapter 2 if necessary) into the cordonnet. Remember to take the thread under and over the side cordonnet twice at the end of the row, so as to have the thread in the correct position for your next row [52].

Continue the rows of double Bruxelles, taking two stitches into each long loop in the row above as you did in your practice sampler. Again, the beauty of this stitch is in its evenness, so keep an eye on the diagonal pattern the pairs of stitches make in the petal. As you did in the sampler, keep the thread straight in the gaps between the groups of pairs of stitches as you work, thus producing even-sized holes.

Increase and decrease as necessary to keep to the outline shape of the petal. You will find that in some rows you will only be able to fit in one of the paired stitches at the ends [53]. This does not matter; it is, in fact, the way you keep the pattern of the stitches correct.

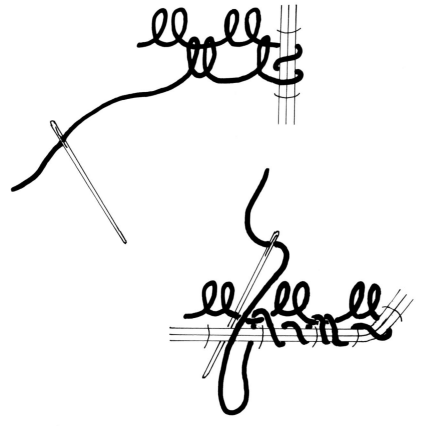

53 *Double Bruxelles stitch: sometimes the space only allows for one of the paired stitches at the ends of rows.*

54 *Petal two: whip the last row down to the cordonnet.*

When the filling is complete, finish by whipping it down to the cordonnet. Take two whipping stitches into each long loop so that the pattern is kept here as well [54], just as you did in the sampler.

Third petal

This petal is worked in the 'lattice-type' filling stitch, (see Chapter 2). It is a very pretty stitch and is quick to work, but you need to be careful to keep the ends of the rows in pattern. Refer back to your sampler if necessary.

Begin at the left, as you did in the first two petals. Work your pairs of buttonhole stitches across to the right, leaving the loops between the groups fairly slack as you did in the practice sampler.

At the end of the row take the thread under the right side cordonnet as usual. Whip once over and under the cordonnet before laying the cord across to the left, so that the cord lies barely touching the long loops of the row above. Take the thread under the left cordonnet as usual.

Whip down the left cordonnet to be in position for the next row. Due to the shaping of the petal, you will need to increase at the beginning and end of this next row. Do this by taking the extra stitches into the cordonnet as usual, but it is very important that you keep the pattern correct [55].

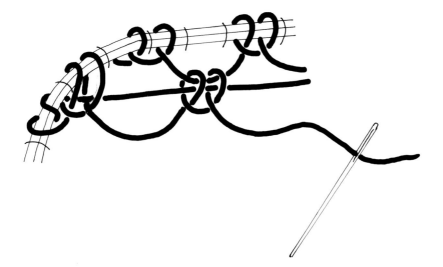

55 *Petal three: increasing at the beginning of a row of 'Lattice-type' filling to keep the correct pattern.*

Continue the filling, increasing and decreasing as necessary, but always keeping the pattern correct. As in your sampler, you will find that sometimes you do not need to whip down the cordonnet before laying the cord. depending on where your row ended [56]. Your practice sampler and the photograph [41] of the motif with its cordonnette worked, will help in this. Everyone's tension is slightly different, so it is not possible to give categoric details. Besides which, it is one of the fascinations of needlepoint lace to work a pattern to fit a certain design outline.

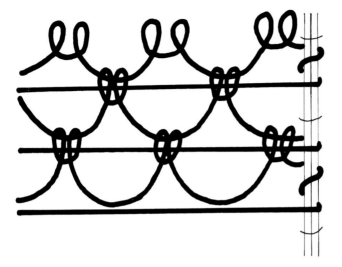

56 *'Lattice-type' filling: pattern at the ends of rows.*

Complete the petal by whipping down the long loops of the last row of stitches to the cordonnet as usual.

Fourth petal
This is worked in whipped single Bruxelles stitch (See Chapter 2). Begin at the left, as you did with the other petals, and work a row of single detached buttonhole stitches across to the right, using the cordonnet. Make each stitch about 3mm ($\frac{1}{8}$in) apart, taking the thread under the cordonnet at the end of the row as usual.

Whip back across the row of loops by taking the needle downwards once through each loop [57]. Go under the cordonnet at the end of this whipping row as usual. It looks neater if the thread comes out at the same point where the first stitch of the row above began. The whipping should also lie almost in a straight line.

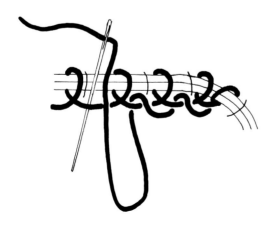

57 *Petal four: whipped single Bruxelles stitch.*

53

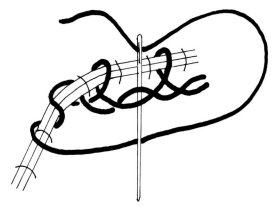

Take the thread under and over the left cordonnet again, so that you are in position for your next row. When you work this and other stitch rows, the needle always passes behind both the loop and the whip stitch on making the stitch [58].

Continue your lace filling, increasing and decreasing as necessary to keep to the shape of the petal. Keep the evenness of this filling by making sure the rows are always the same distance apart, so that the lace works up like brickwork.

Complete by whipping the last row down to the cordonnet at the end. You do not need to work the whipping row before you do this.

The lace fillings of your petals are now all completed. Before you work your buttonholed cordonnette around the edges, a decorative 'wheel' may be worked in the centre space. Do not cut your lace from the foundation until the wheel centre and cordonnette are completed.

Wheel centre

There are a variety of 'wheels' in needlepoint lace, the simplest of which is given here. Another is given in the first variation motif at the end of this chapter.

Using a length of Number 40 crochet cotton and the ball-pointed needle, fasten on to the cordonnet at the centre of the base of the first petal. Take the thread immediately across to the centre of the base of petal three opposite and take the needle under and over the cordonnet here. Make two whipping stitches back along this thread, so as to be at the centre of the thread. Without pulling the thread out of place, take the needle under the cordonnet at the centre of the base of petal four [59].

Again make two whipping stitches back along this thread to the centre, then take the thread straight across and under the cordonnet of the opposite petal [60]. Make two whipping stitches back to the centre along this thread.

You are now at the centre. All the legs, except for the first, have been whip-stitched.

54

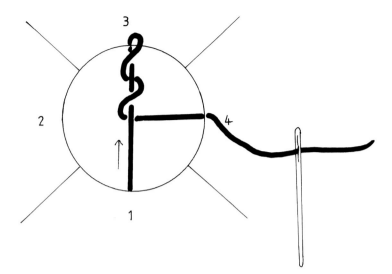

59 *Wheel centre*
(1).

To make the central wheel, weave under and over around this centre twice, having started and ended by the unwhipped leg. Do not pull up tightly since all the threads should be seen clearly in the wheel pattern.

Make two whipping stitches down the first leg, which had been left

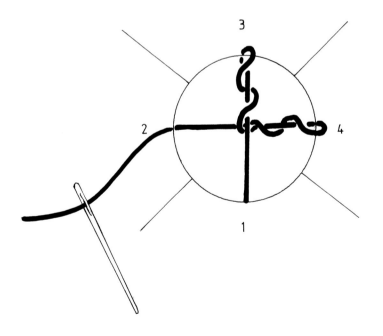

60 *Wheel centre*
(2).

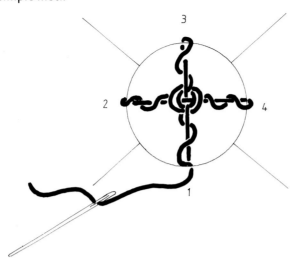

unwhipped [61]. Fasten off at the cordonnet if your working thread is rather short. A word of warning – it is very easy to pull the thread too tightly when fastening off, turning your wheel into a knot!

If the thread is still quite long, do not end it off completely. Instead, make a single fastening buttonhole stitch and run it under the stitches on the cordonnet, until your reach a suitable position (1 on the original motif diagram) for beginning your buttonholed cordonnette around the edges of the petals.

The cordonnette

This gives the 'finish' to the piece of lace. It consists of blanket or simple detached buttonhole stitches worked around the outlines of the completed motif, the centre circle being worked last.

The buttonhole stitches of the cordonnette in this motif are worked over a doubled strand of thread, which is laid over the cordonnet, but not couched down. (See Chapter 2.) These stitches, and the threads laid under them, are worked in the thread used for the lace filling stitches, namely Number 40 crochet cotton.

The doubled-over thread, which is to be laid over the cordonnet, should be sufficiently long to go around all the outlines of the design. In this motif it will be approximately 100cm (40in) of Number 40 crochet cotton, folded over to give the doubled thread of 50cm (20in) length.

Petal one

Using a ball-pointed needle and a normal length of Number 40 crochet cotton, fasten on in the usual manner at 1 (see original motif diagram). You will then be ready to work around the edge of the first petal, turning your work around as necessary.

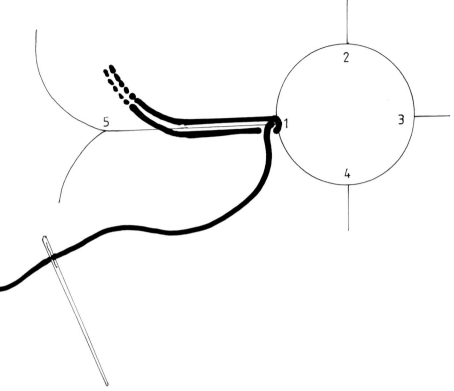

To start, bring the needle through the loop of the doubled thread [62], which you will lay exactly over the cordonnet. Work the simple detached buttonhole stitches quite closely around the edge of the first petal until you reach 6.

The stitches enclose the cordonnet edge and laid threads. Take care that you do not pass through the surface of the acetate covering your design. The 'loops' of the stitches lie towards the outside. If you are right-handed it is best to work the stitches towards yourself from right to left, so that your left hand can hold the laid threads in position as you work. In this way the design will be upside-down when you start the cordonnette of this first petal. Turn the work as necessary as you proceed.

Make sure that you do not accidentally disarrange the position of stitches at the ends of the rows while working the cordonnette. However, this is a useful opportunity to re-arrange stitches if necessary. Even if you do not normally use a thimble, you will find it a great help here.

When you reach the junction at 6, take the inner laid thread down to the cordonnet circle at 2. To anchor the thread, take it under the cordonnet here. Then bring it out and back to join the other laid thread at 6, so that you can continue it around the next petal. This is very similar to the method you have already used to work branches in the original cordonnet outline.

Making a simple motif

Work petal one so that it appears to overlap the second petal. Continue the buttonhole stitches around the edge of this first petal (over the threads you have just laid) down to 2 on the centre circle [63]. Fasten off the working thread here.

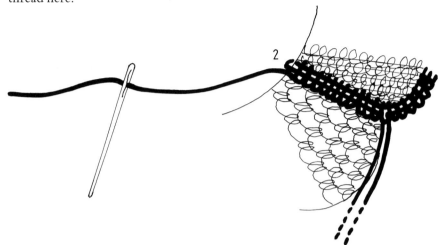

63 *Petal one overlapping petal two: the buttonhole 'loops' on the outside of petal one.*

If you had wanted petal two to appear on top of the first petal, you would only work the buttonholing as far as the junction at 6. You would then lay the inner laid thread down and back as usual, but you would also take the working thread down to the centre circle at 2. You would then begin the buttonholing of petal two starting from here, so that the 'loops' were towards the outside edge of this petal [64]. In this way, you are able to choose which petals you want to appear more prominent.

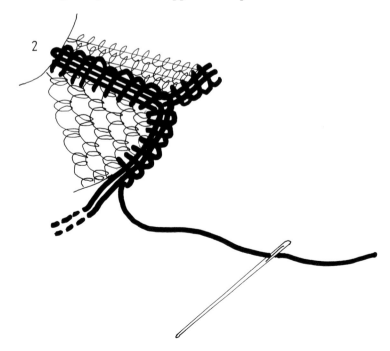

64 *Alternative variation: petal two appearing to overlap petal one.*

Petal two
Fasten on a new working thread. The two laid threads are there already. It is obviously neater if any fastening on or off lies under the laid threads.

First, take the needle through the nearest adjacent buttonhole loop of petal one for continuity [65], then work the buttonholing around the second petal as far as the branch at 7.

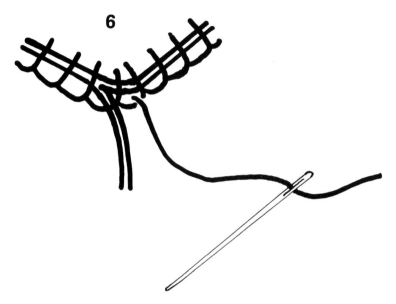

6

65 *Commencing the cordonnette for petal two.*

Petal two lies under the third one. Using the method previously described, take the inner laid thread down to the centre circle at 3 and back to rejoin its pair. Take the working thread down to 3 as well, and make a fastening buttonhole stitch, but do not cut if off.

Petal three
Work the buttonholing up the petal edge; the loops will be on the outside of this petal. Continue this buttonholing around the rest of the petal.

The third petal lies over the fourth. At junction 8, follow the method you used at junction 6. Fasten off the working thread at 4.

Petal four
The fourth petal lies under both the third and first petals. Fasten on your working thread at 8, remembering to go through an adjacent loop, and buttonhole along the top edge of the petal.

End off the cordonnette when you reach 5 by cutting off the two laid threads closely. Work one further buttonhole stitch to cover the ends. Take the needle through the most immediate loop of the cordonnette of the first petal. End off this working thread with a tight buttonhole stitch and run the thread under the cordonnette a short way before cutting it off.

The centre circle

Only the cordonnette of the centre circle remains to be worked. Usually the loops of the cordonnette buttonholing lie on the outside edges, but here they look better if worked towards the petals [41].

Various 'finishes' can be used for this centre circle, the simplest being the plain cordonnette. In this motif, the centre's buttonholing stitches are worked over four laid threads to achieve a slight increase in thickness. Estimate the length of the laid threads here in the usual manner.

Fasten the working thread anywhere on the centre circle. Work your cordonnette buttonholing right around the circle, this time over four laid threads, the first stitch passing through the two loops of the doubled laid threads. Make the 'loops' of the buttonhole stitches lie towards the outside of the flower.

To complete, take the needle through the loop of the first buttonhole stitch, thus linking the circle of stitches. End off as usual.

Removal from the backing

Take out the tacking stitches around the design and the foundation so that you can part the calico foundation layers. The lace is held by the cordonnet couching stitches. Never try to cut the lace free from the top. Instead, just part the calico layers and cut the couching stitches, which can be seen clearly between these layers.

Gently lift the covered design (with the lace) off the calico. Remove any visible couching threads from the underside of the design and then lift the lace from the design. This avoids unnecessary straining on the lace. Tweezers are very useful for this. Remove any extra couching threads from the back of the motif.

Washing

Should you need to clean the finished motif, it can be washed gently by hand in ordinary washing powder, provided the threads are washable. Rinse well and pat gently with a tissue or towel to remove excess water. Lay the motif on a towel to dry flat.

Uses

Your motif can be displayed in various ways. Mine was made into a paperweight, but it could also be used to decorate fabric box lids, glass drinks coasters and powder-box lids, or mounted in a frame – many craft shops stock suitable mounts.

Paperweight

To decorate a paperweight 9cm ($3\frac{1}{2}$in) in diameter, cut out a circle of sueded velvet-type contact backing to fit the *inner* base of the paperweight. (I find it best to keep the paper backing on this piece.) Position the motif on it and place under the paperweight.

Finally, cut another circle of the backing 9cm ($3\frac{1}{2}$in) in diameter, remove the paper backing and press the contact side over the back of the paperweight.

Other fabrics can be used under the glass to match your furnishings.

Variations

This first motif has taken you through all the basic stages involved in working a simple piece of needlepoint lace. It is enjoyable to be able to use your own ideas to design and develop a piece of lace. Although I like to see lace displayed, equally I like to use it on linens and clothes. The two variations given here should stimulate you to experiment with your own designs.

Inserted motif

The motif has been inserted into the corner of a table napkin, by using the cordonnette to attach the motif to the material. It could also be made into an insert for a pocket on a linen-type skirt or dress, with the colours either matched to the material or contrasted. It is advisable to choose compatible weights of threads and fabrics, making sure that both wash or dry-clean well

66 *Inserted daisy motif.*

61

and the fabric is suitable. There are several ways of attaching lace to fabric, but this one uses the actual cordonnette buttonholing stitches.

The motif was worked in Numbers 20 and 60 crochet cottons. You can either use the same stitches as in the first motif, or try out some of those given in Chapter 4. This one contains corded Bruxelles, double Bruxelles and the 'lattice-type' filling stitch, together with a petal in the corded Bruxelles with two four-hole diamonds and a row of twisted Bruxelles. Instructions for the decorative centre looped cordonnette are given in detail in Chapter 5.

Method
Work the motif in the following stages:

1 Using the same motif diagram, couch down a cordonnet of Number 20 crochet cotton.
2 Work the lace filling stitches in Number 60 crochet cotton.
3 Work a centre wheel (see Chapter 4 if you wish to work the buttonholed wheel).
4 Remove the lace from the calico foundation and design as usual.
    Note: You have not yet worked the cordonnette.
5 Place the motif in position on the right side of your chosen item, for example, a table napkin, and tack it firmly.
6 Place the napkin in a small embroidery hoop, or re-tack onto the design and calico backing.
7 Work the cordonnette around the edges of the petals as in the original motif, using Number 60 crochet cotton. The buttonhole stitches should be worked right through the napkin fabric as well. In this way, the cordonnette is used to join the lace to the napkin.
8 Work the centre circle cordonnette.
9 Remove the napkin from your embroidery hoop, or from the foundation.
10 Carefully cut away the napkin fabric from behind the motif, making sure that you do not cut the lace itself. The cordonnette prevents any fraying. If the material is very loosely woven, the lace could be machine zig-zag stitched into position as an extra precaution at stage 5 before working the cordonnette.

Reduced size with added raised petals

This looks particularly lovely on a handkerchief corner or a blouse. The added embroidery is an extra creative touch, which you can adapt to suit your own design. The design is smaller, which means you must obviously use thinner threads.

The handkerchief corner shown was worked completely in pink Brillante

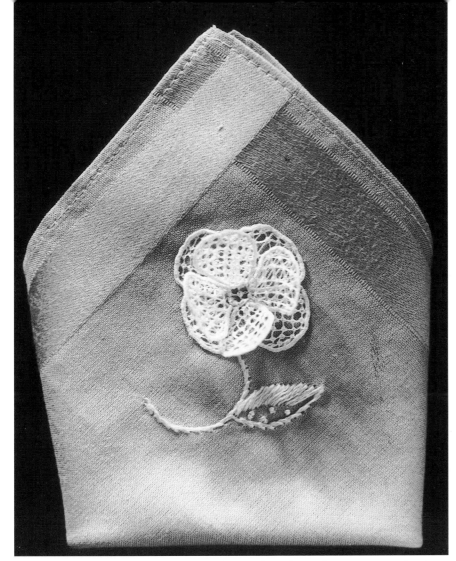

d'Alsace cotton Number 50, with added embroidery using two strands of green embroidery thread, on a lilac-coloured cotton hankie. Ordinary sewing cotton could be used instead of the Brillante d'Alsace if wished. The stitches are made to appear light and delicate, using only double Bruxelles and the 'lattice-type' filling stitches.

As a further refinement, petals are added to the original motif to give a 3-D effect. These petals are worked as separate pieces and added to the motif later.

Method

Work your lace in the following stages:

1 Using the hankie design for the small motif and petals [68], couch the cordonnet of Number 50 Brillante d'Alsace cotton around the outlines of the motif. End off and work the cordonnet of each petal separately.

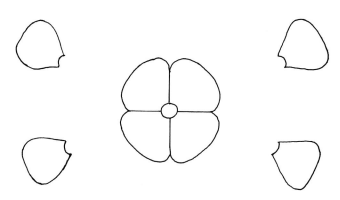

2 Work the lace filling stitches in Number 50 Brillante d'Alsace cotton. The hankie motif illustrated used alternating petals of double Bruxelles and 'lattice-type' stitch.

3 Work the centre wheel.

4 Buttonhole the cordonnette around the outlines of the motif and petals. Omit the small area at the base of each separate petal [69] as well as the centre circle of the motif.

69 *Cordonnette of a single petal.*

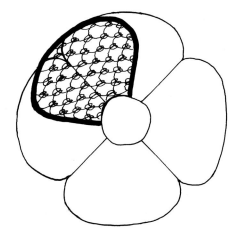

70 *Positioning petals on the worked motif. For clarity, only the lace stitches in the petal are indicated.*

5 Remove the separate petals from the backing, leaving the motif in position. Do not remove this yet.
6 Tack the separate petals in position on the motif. It will look attractive if each petal lies over the 'join' of the motif petals [70].
7 Work the centre circle cordonnette through both layers of lace, i.e. motif and top petals.
8 Remove from the foundation backing.
9 Tack and stitch the lace into position on the hankie. Remember the stitches on the back should not show too much.
10 Embroider a stem and leaves onto the material using two strands of embroidery thread.

The beautiful Point de Gaze collar shown [71] has added petals. The cordonnette of these separate petals is worked completely around each petal, then they are stab-stitched in position when the lace is finished.

71 *Point de Gaze (mid-nineteenth century): end of a collar belonging to the author.*

four

More stitches and 'sampler' projects

This chapter shows you how to work a further selection of needlepoint lace stitches. They can be tried out on your original sampler using the Number 40 crochet cotton, or worked into one of the 'sampler' ideas at the end of this chapter which use different thread.

Twisted single Bruxelles stitch

This is like the basic single Bruxelles stitch, but with an extra twist [72]. Fasten on at the left slightly lower than usual – a little more than 3mm ($\frac{1}{8}$in) down. Take your thread to the right and back again to make a small loop – I hold it with my left forefinger – then take the needle down into the top tape (or under the top cordonnet) as usual, about 3mm ($\frac{1}{8}$in) away [73].

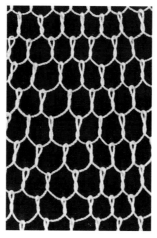

72 *Twisted single Bruxelles stitch.*

Take the needle 'into' the loop by going over the higher thread of the loop and under the lower one [74]. Draw up the stitch gently.

Work the next stitch about 3mm ($\frac{1}{8}$in) away from the first, making sure

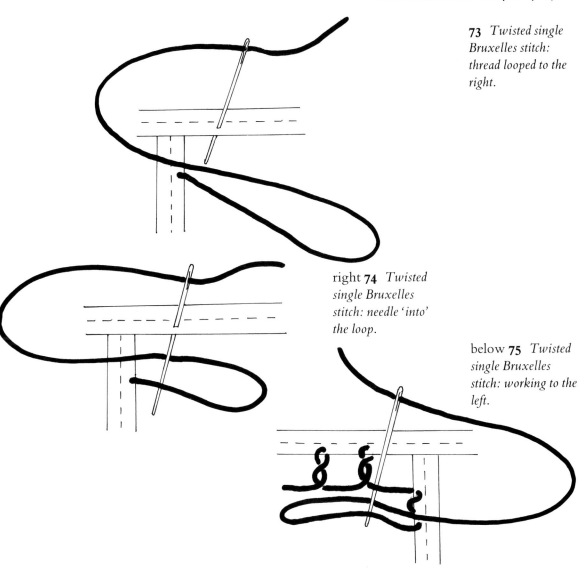

73 *Twisted single Bruxelles stitch: thread looped to the right.*

right **74** *Twisted single Bruxelles stitch: needle 'into' the loop.*

below **75** *Twisted single Bruxelles stitch: working to the left.*

that the loop between the stitches lies straight, so that there is a 'box-like' shape to the space. Continue to the end of the row. Take the needle under and into the side tape (or under the cordonnet), just over 3mm ($\frac{1}{8}$in) down from the top. Whip it down once or twice so that you are at the correct depth for the next row, which will be equal to the depth of the twisted single Bruxelles stitch.

The stitches of this next and every successive row are worked into the loops between the stitches of the row above. Since this row is worked from right to left, each stitch is made by taking the thread to the left, and then back to the right to make the loop when working the stitch [75].

When drawing up the stitches, I find it best to put the tip of my needle into the top part of the stitch as I ease it up into position [76]. This avoids pulling and distorting the stitches of the row above.

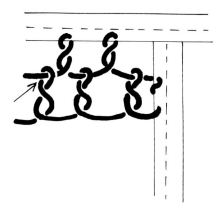

76 *Twisted single Bruxelles stitch: easing stitch into position.*

Should you find this stitch difficult, a similar effect can be achieved by taking the needle directly upwards, under and into the tape [77]. Next, pass the

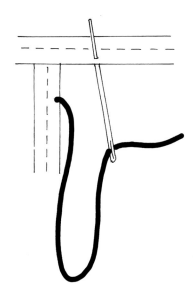

77 *Twisted single Bruxelles stitch: alternative method, needle up under tape.*

needle back up through this loop and gently pull up the stitch formed [78]. However, the twist on the stitch will lie in the opposite direction, which is not really correct. This stitch can be worked in rows in both directions, you just think to yourself 'up and up' as you work each stitch.

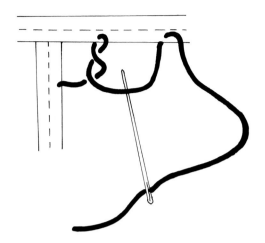

78 *Twisted single Bruxelles stitch: alternative method, needle up through the loop.*

An area can be filled completely with rows of twisted single Bruxelles stitches, or the stitches can be used in a variety of ways to give different patterns.

Single row of twisted single Bruxelles in a corded stitch area

For this particular variation, refer to illustration 25. Work rows of corded single Bruxelles stitch as shown in Chapter 2, until you are at the point where you want to work a row of the twisted single Bruxelles, ending with the 'stitch' row of the corded stitch. In order to be at the correct depth for beginning your row of twisted single Bruxelles, whip once or twice down the cordonnet.

Each stitch is worked into alternate loops. Therefore, miss the first loop of the corded stitch row above and make your first single twisted Bruxelles stitch into the next loop. Work across the row in this manner, taking a stitch into every alternate loop [79]. At the end of the row take the thread under the cordonnet as usual.

79 *A row of twisted single Bruxelles in a corded stitch area: working into alternate loops.*

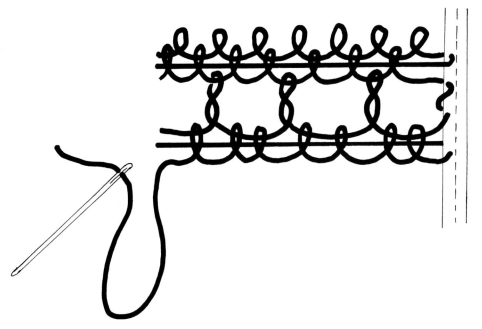

80 *A row of twisted single Bruxelles in a corded stitch area: continuing the corded stitch.*

Continue with the rows of corded single Bruxelles stitch. I prefer to lay a cord immediately after the row of twisted Bruxelles as it gives a firmer appearance. Because you have just worked the twisted stitches into alternate loops, you will now have to work two stitches into each long loop to get back to the original number [80].

Each stitch of this row will obviously enclose the long loops of the twisted Bruxelles row, as well as the cord just laid. You will also notice that you are now working your corded stitch rows in the other direction.

An effective pattern can be made by working 'bands' of three or four rows of corded single Bruxelles stitch with a row of twisted single Bruxelles stitch between each band.

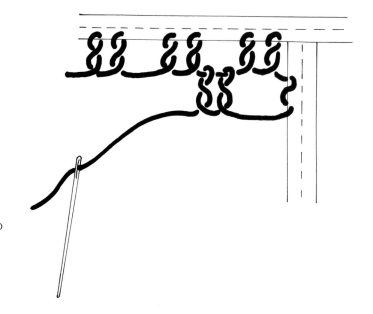

81 *Twisted Bruxelles stitch: doubles.*

Working groups of twisted Bruxelles stitches

The stitches can be worked as doubles [81] or trebles. In each, the gap
between the groups is equal in length to the space taken by the number of
stitches in each group.

Whipped twisted single Bruxelles stitch

Each row of twisted single Bruxelles stitch is whipped, using the method for
the ordinary whipped Bruxelles stitch in Chapter 2 [82]. First, work a row of
twisted single Bruxelles stitches, ending by bringing the needle out through
the tape (or under the cordonnet) at the end of the row.

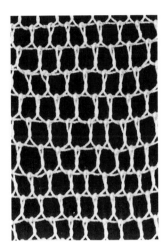

82 Whipped twisted single Bruxelles stitch.

Whip immediately across to the other side by taking one whip stitch into
each loop. End by taking the needle under and out at the same point as the
first stitch of the row above [83].

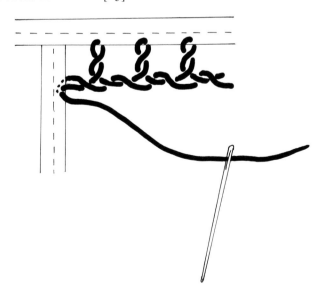

83 Whipped twisted single Bruxelles stitch.

71

Whip down once or twice, to be at the correct position for the next row of twisted Bruxelles stitch. In working this and successive stitch rows, the needle passes behind two threads when making the twisted stitch, i.e. behind the loop and its whip stitch.

If you pull the whipped thread gently but firmly as you work it, so that it lies in a straight line, you will achieve a 'box-like' mesh, very similar to Burano mesh.

If you whip twice into each stitch and leave the whipped thread slightly slacker, then the rows of twisted stitches will pull the lace filling into a hexagonal-shaped mesh, similar to a type of Alençon lace mesh.

Pea stitch

This consists of alternate rows of double Bruxelles and single Bruxelles stitches [84]. First, fasten on at the left tape in the usual position near the top and work a row of double Bruxelles across to the right. At the end of the row take the needle under and out through the right hand tape (or under the cordonnet), and whip down once to be at a stitch depth ready for the next row.

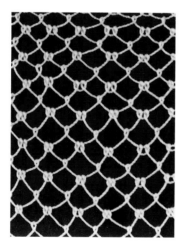

84 *Pea stitch.*

Work a row to the left consisting of single Bruxelles stitches, each worked into the long loop between the groups of doubles. At the end of the row take the needle under and out through the tape and again whip down once to be at the right depth for the next row, which consists of double Bruxelles stitches worked into the long loops [85]. Continue your filling, alternating these two rows.

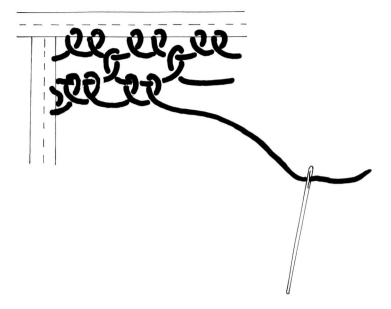

85 *Pea stitch.*

Pea stitch variation

There are several variations, but this is a very pretty one, which is found in many of the old Venetian laces [86]. It consists of two basic rows.

Fasten on at the left and work a row of double Bruxelles stitches into the top tape. Leave a slightly longer gap between each group equal in distance to the space occupied by three stitches. Keep the thread straight between each pair. At the end of the row bring the thread under and out through the tape. Whip down it once before starting the next row.

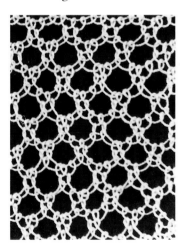

86 *Pea stitch variation.*

Work a row of single Bruxelles stitches across the row to the left, taking one stitch into the small loops between the pairs of double stitches, and three

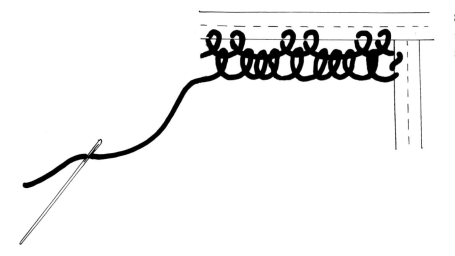

87 *Pea stitch variation: second row.*

stitches into the longer loops between them [87]. At the end, again whip down the tape once to be at the correct position for the next row. **Think of this row as a continuous row of evenly spaced stitches. This will give you a neater effect**.

This next row is the same as the first, but take the group of two stitches into the loops which lie between the three stitches which you worked into the long loops [88]. In effect you are making two stitches, leaving two loops, making two stitches, and so on. Remember to keep the thread straight between the groups of pairs. At the end of the row, whip down the tape as before.

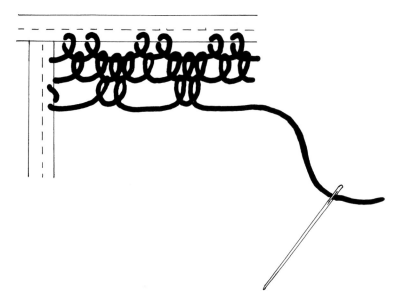

88 *Pea stitch variations: third row.*

74

The next row is worked exactly as the second. Sometimes you will not be able to fit all three stitches into the loop at the ends of the rows; just work one or two as desired.

Continue the lace filling, working the two basic rows so that the holes create a 'brickwork' as they alternate. This pea stitch variation may be worked quite closely, or it may be spaced so that a looser effect is achieved. If you are working the filling in a shaped area, increase or decrease at the beginning or end of the rows as necessary, but keep the pattern correct. On completing the filling stitches in the area, remember to whip the final rows down in such a way that the lace is kept in pattern.

Decorative holes or slits in corded stitch

Decorative patterns can be made in an area of corded single Bruxelles or corded stitch by working holes, or longer slits, either singly or in groups [92].

A single small hole
To make a single small hole, work in corded stitch until you are just above the position where you wish to make the hole, having just laid the cord.

Work the stitch row across until you are at the position where you want the hole. Leaving two loops unworked, continue the stitches to complete the row, and again lay the cord as usual [89].

89 *Single small hole in corded stitch: leaving two loops unworked.*

Work a row of stitches to the point where you left the two unworked loops. To complete the hole, work *three* stitches with the needle passing behind the three threads which lie at the position of the hole [90]. As you had

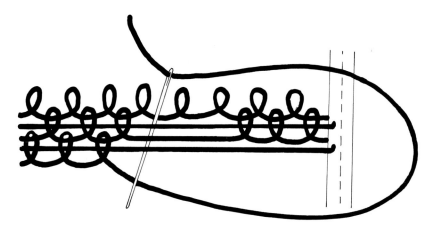

90 *Single small hole in corded stitch: work three stitches in the space with the needle behind the three straight threads.*

left two unworked loops in the first stage, you have to make three stitches here to get you back to the correct number of loops. You always need to work one extra number of stitches to loops in order to achieve this. Three stitches give you two loops, four stitches would give you three loops, and so on. Work to the end of the row in the usual manner. Now, lay the cord across and continue with your corded stitch filling [91].

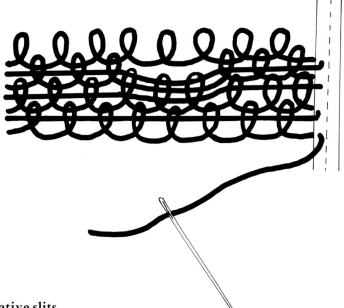

91 *Completed single small hole in an area of corded stitch (corded Bruxelles).*

Decorative slits
These are worked in exactly the same way as the small hole, but you leave more loops unworked, depending on the length of the slit desired. Again, remember to work one more stitch than the number of loops; if, for example, you left four unworked loops, then you will need to make five stitches over the three threads in the space left.

Four-hole diamond

This is worked as four small holes in a similar manner [92], and is a common feature of some of the old Venetian laces. Work in corded stitch until you are just above the position of the top hole (having laid the cord as usual).

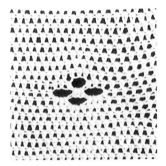

92 Four-hole diamond in corded stitch.

Work your stitches across the next row to the point where you wish to make the top hole. Leave two loops unworked and continue to the end of the row, just as you would when making a single small hole [93]. Now lay the cord across to the other side as usual.

93 Four-hole diamond in corded stitch: leaving two loops for the top hole.

The next row will contain the unworked loops of the next two holes on each side of the completed top hole. Work your row of stitches across this row until you are two loops before your previous missed loops. Leave these two loops unworked then complete the top hole by making three stitches into the space left (remembering that you are making the stitches pass behind three threads here). Miss the next two loops and continue your stitches to the end [94]. Lay the cord across to the other side as usual.

94 Four-hole diamond in corded stitch: completing the top hole and leaving the loops for the two side holes.

The next row completes the two side holes and begins the final lower hole of the diamond. Work across the row until you reach the first two unworked loops; complete the hole here by working three stitches into the space, again over three threads. Miss the next two loops (these will form your last hole in the diamond). Complete the next hole by working three

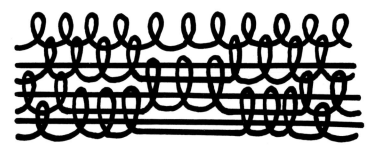

95 *Four-hole diamond in corded stitch: completing the side holes and leaving loops for the lower hole.*

stitches into the space, then continue your row to the end [95]. Lay the cord across to the other side.

This row completes the four-hole diamond pattern. Work across the row to the point where you missed the two loops for your last hole. Work three stitches here over the three threads and work to the end of the row [96]. Lay the cord across and continue your area of corded stitch.

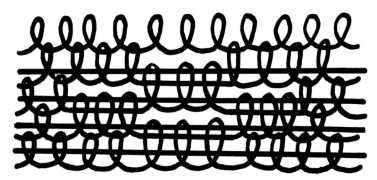

96 *Four-hole diamond in corded stitch: completing the diamond.*

Instructions have been given in detail, to enable you to try a nine-hole diamond yourself [97] if you wish. It is worked on the same basic principle.

97 *Arrangement of holes in a nine-hole diamond.*

Remember to keep the ends of the rows level and fractionally pulled down so that the 'holes' open out when completed. If you find you have worked a hole with a thread left across it, the reason is that you did not work your stitches over all three threads in the space. It happens to most of us sooner or later!

Double point de Venise

This pretty stitch variation is really made up of the double Bruxelles stitch you already know, with two simple buttonhole stitches worked sideways, back over the loop between this group and the last [98].

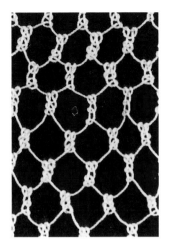

98 *Double point de Venise.*

Fasten on at the left tape or cordonnet near the top. Leave a space equivalent to two stitches – using Number 40 crochet cotton in the sampler this would be about 0.5cm ($\frac{1}{4}$in) – then work a single simple buttonhole stitch, leave another space and continue across the row. This forms a foundation row for the actual stitches.

At the end of this row whip twice down the right-hand tape or cordonnet so that you are ready to begin the first row of stitches, about 0.5cm ($\frac{1}{4}$in) below the foundation row, working to the left.

Work two simple buttonhole stitches into the first long loop, leaving the thread behind them slightly slack. With the needle pointing to the left, work a buttonhole stitch into this loop [99]. It will sit just below the double stitch

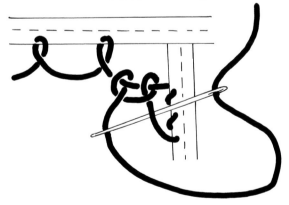

99 *Double point de Venise: beginning the first stitch into the foundation row.*

with the 'knot' towards the left. Work another sideways buttonhole stitch below the first [100]. As you work each stitch in the group of double point de Venise, ease it into position gently.

Leaving the thread slightly slack between each group, continue to work a double point de Venise into each of the long loops of the foundation row. At

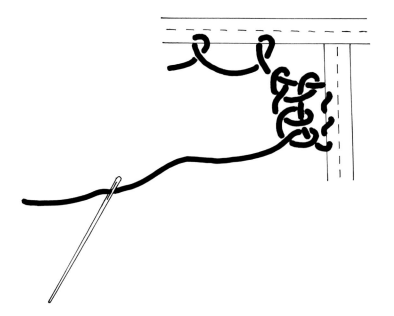

100 *Double point de Venise stitch: working towards the left.*

the end of the row take the thread under and out through the tape 0.5cm ($\frac{1}{4}$in) below the top to keep both ends of the row even.

If you look at the photograph [98] of this stitch you will see it forms hexagonal patterns. To keep it regular, try to make the six sides of the hexagon look equal in length.

Whip twice down the left tape to be in position to work your next row of double point de Venise stitches.

Work a double point de Venise into each long loop of the row above, again leaving the loop between each group slightly slack. When you work to the right, as in this row, the 'knots' of the two sideways stitches point to the right, since they are made with the needle pointing to the right [101].

Continue working rows of double point de Venise alternately towards the left and right, remembering to watch the pattern at the ends of the rows so as to keep the 'hexagons' looking correct. This pretty double stitch is a variation of the basic single petit point de Venise stitch, which consists of a single simple buttonhole stitch with one sideways stitch.

Point de Venise has other variations, one of which is the cinq point stitch.

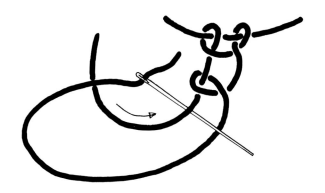

101 *Double point de Venise stitch: working towards the right.*

Cinq point de Venise or shell stitch

This is an extremely useful stitch. When worked in fine thread it makes
delicate sidways groups; in thick threads the stitch gives an interesting
'knobbly' texture to modern lace designs [102].

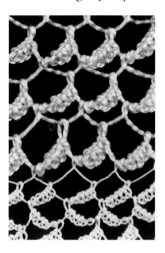

102 *Cinq point de
Venise: worked in
thick and thin
threads.*

In this stitch fasten on at the right and make a foundation row, as you did
in the double point de Venise stitch above, but working to the left. Whip
down the left tape once only to be ready for the first row of cinq point stitch.

Make a single buttonhole stitch into the first long loop of the foundation
row above, but do not pull it up completely. You need to have enough space
to work five buttonhole stitches into the loop left behind it.

Hold the thread in place with your left forefinger. Keeping the point of
the needle facing down slightly to the right, take the thread down in a loop
and make the first of the five buttonhole stitches into the lower end of the
loop, the needle passing behind the two threads [103]. **This one forms a**

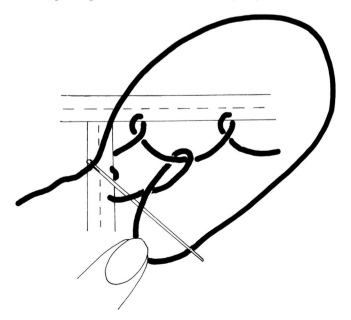

103 *Cinq point de
Venise: making the
first of the five
buttonhole stitches.*

sort of 'knot' holding the cinq point in position, so make sure it is in the right place before you tighten it up. I use the point of the needle to help ease it into place.

The five buttonhole stitches in this cinq point stitch are worked from the bottom of the loop to the top, unlike those worked in the double point de Venise stitch above. Work four more buttonhole stitches into the loop, the last of which should sit below the single straight stitch.

Continue the row, working a cinq point stitch group into each long loop of the foundation row. The single straight stitch should be placed in the centre of the loop to keep the effect.

At the end of the row take the thread under and out of the right-hand tape at the same level as the start of the row. Whip once down the tape if necessary.

Working to the left, make a single buttonhole stitch into the loop at the base of the cinq point groups [104]. Leave the thread between each stitch just fractionally slacker than in a normal single Bruxelles row. Take the thread under and out through the left tape. Whip it down once so that you are ready to start the next row of cinq point stitches.

Work a row of cinq point stitch groups to the right. Each is worked into the long loop between the single stitches as before. Continue the pattern by alternately working rows of single stitches and rows of cinq point stitch groups.

Cinq point stitch can be worked in alternate rows as above, or as successive rows which are worked in both directions. The cinq point of the right and left rows will then lie in opposite directions.

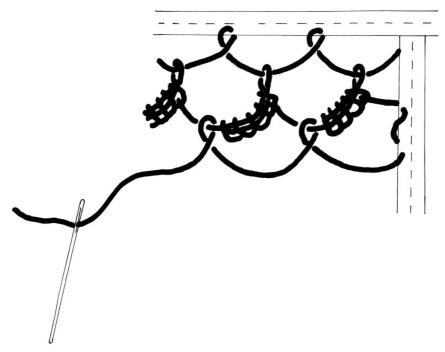

104 *Cinq point de Venise worked with alternate rows of single Bruxelles stitch.*

Wheel-filling

This can be worked as a single row in a narrow space, as well as within a larger area [105]. The instructions for the latter are given here, since it looks very effective this way. I recommend trying it out first in one of the sampler areas.

The 'wheels' are worked on a mesh of diagonally crossing threads. The first set of diagonal threads are laid as doubles (but using a single working thread), then the other set of crossing threads are laid singly. Your wheels are worked after the laying of each single thread by working back along it.

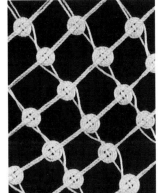

105 *Wheel-filling.*

Using your sampler square, fasten on the working thread to the left tape about 1cm ($\frac{3}{8}$in) down from the top. Lay the thread diagonally up to the right, taking your needle down into and out from the top tape about 1cm ($\frac{3}{8}$in) along from the left edge. Now go back down to the point where you started. Take the needle under and out of the left tape here, just fractionally below the first thread. You have just made the first of the double diagonal threads. I find that this way of laying the threads keeps them lying together and not crossing over each other.

Whip down the tape. Then continue laying the double diagaonals 1cm ($\frac{3}{8}$in) apart until you have laid the last one near to the bottom right-hand corner. Whip along the left tape and the lower tape as necessary [106].

Whip along the tape to the bottom right-hand corner of the square so that you can lay the first of the single threads from this corner. This provides a guide for keeping the others equidistant.

Take your thread from the bottom right corner straight over to the top left corner, and bring the needle down into and out of the tape here. Your single thread should be at right angles to the double ones it lies over.

You are now ready to work your wheels back down this single thread. Make sure that you have enough thread to work all the wheels along this thread. You cannot join on in the middle.

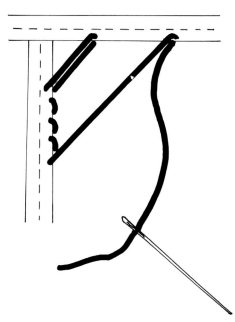

106 *Wheel-filling: laying the double diagonal threads.*

I like to work the first row at the centre like this, so that I can judge the pattern better, but you can also commence with a short row near the left-hand corner.

Bring the thread back down to the point where the single thread crossed the first double one. Make a wheel here by weaving clockwise two or three times around this crossing. Always take the thread *under* the two original laid doubles, and *over* the singles, keeping the threads of the wheel in position. This is very similar to the wheel which was made at the centre of the first daisy motif.

The next wheel is worked in an anti-clockwise direction. You will see that the thread almost takes itself on the right path to the next wheel. Continue working the wheels along this line [107]. Work each one alternately clockwise and anti-clockwise. The wheels should not be so large that they touch each other.

After working the last wheel in this line, take the thread to the bottom tape by the side of the laid single thread. Whip 1cm (just over ¼in) along the tape to the position for laying the next equidistant single. Work this as before, making the wheels back along it. Continue until you have filled the area.

As the wheels of a row are woven in alternate directions, make sure that the wheel of one row is worked in the opposite direction to the one in the row next to it. This seems to give a neater appearance [105].

You can also work variations, for example, by having alternating large and small wheels, or buttonholing the wheels (see below) as you make each

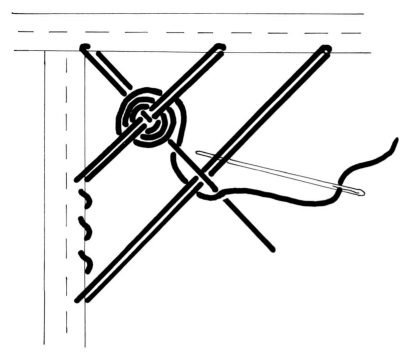

107 *Wheel-filling: working the wheels.*

one. The threads can be laid more closely, especially if fine thread is used, but the wheels should not touch each other. You may also prefer to lay your foundation threads so that you work the wheels upwards away from you.

Buttonholed wheels

Follow the instructions for ordinary wheel-filling until you reach the point where you are ready to work your wheels along the single thread. Work one wheel in the normal way. There are four rays coming from the wheel; think

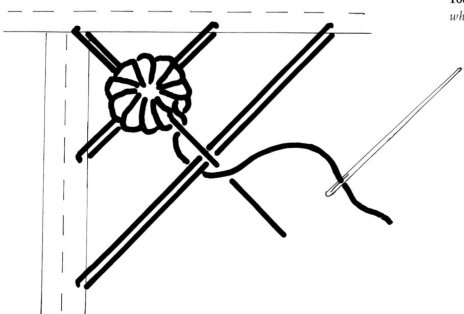

108 *Buttonholed wheel-filling.*

85

of the wheel in quarters and work three or four buttonhole stitches from the centre into each quarter [108].

Since you need to continue on to the next wheel, you must make sure that you start your buttonholing in the correct quarter. Your thread must end in the right place so that you can continue to make the next wheel in your row as usual. Now make the next wheel in the row, and then buttonhole around it as before.

This buttonholing can also be worked for a single wheel at the centre of a motif, as in the buttonholed centre wheel of the insert daisy motif. (See Chapter 3.) Again you need to make sure that you commence and end the buttonholing of the wheel in the correct place. You should finish right next to the unwhipped first leg [109], so that you can whip along this leg to the cordonnet of the circle to fasten off.

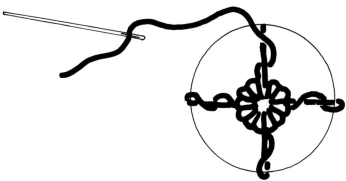

109 *A buttonholed wheel centre.*

Projects

These Christmas tree decorations, as well as the cushion cover described later, are sampler ideas which not only give you practice, but are useful as well. The two shapes illustrated [110] will give you a basis for creating your own decoration designs. Both are particularly effective if worked in irridescent or glittery metallic-effect threads. These two were, in fact, worked in Madeira Metallic-effect Yarn (diamond shape) and Gütermann Metallisiert (round shape), using the 'lattice-type' filling stitch from Chapter 2. However, other stitches may be used instead.

Diamond Christmas tree decoration
This is actually worked as a square-shaped sampler which is then turned to give a diamond.

Materials for each diamond
- 25cm (10in) medium-thick rustless wire
- Irridescent or metallic-effect thread (medium thickness)

- Folded calico foundation backing
- Adhesive acetate film (to colour-contrast with the thread)

110 *Christmas tree decorations.*

Method

1 Trace the square design pattern [111] onto plain paper, cover it with the adhesive film and tack it onto your foundation.
2 Cover your length of wire with the chosen thread by twisting the thread

111 *Square design pattern for the diamond decoration.*

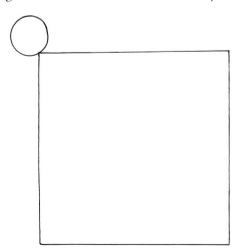

87

tightly around it all along its length. You will find it easier to do this, once you have started it off, if you hold the thread still and twirl the wire between your fingers.

When you reach the last 2cm ($\frac{3}{4}$in), overlap the two ends and wrap the thread over both. Do this very tightly so that it does not come undone later. A dab of clear adhesive will hold the thread in position here if necessary. There is no need to end off the thread, just secure it well with a knot and use it to work your lace filling stitches.

3 Shape your covered wire to fit the square design. The doubled part of the covered wire should be twisted to form the hanging loop at the corner [112]. Instead of laying a normal cordonnet, you couch your covered wire down to the design with ordinary sewing thread.

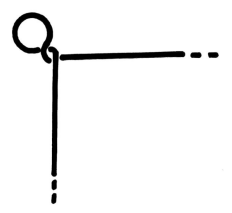

112 *Loop formed by twisting the wire.*

4 Using the chosen thread, work your lace filling stitches in the square with a ball-pointed needle, just as if it were an ordinary sampler square.

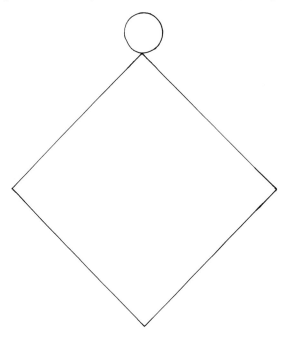

113 *Completed square turned to form the diamond-shape decoration.*

When using metallic threads, it is easier to thread the needle with a needle threader. Instead of whipping your last row down to the lower wire, you could work this last row onto the lower wire for anchorage.

5 The cordonnet framework consists of the covered wire, so you do not have to buttonhole a cordonnette. Remove the square from the design and calico backing by cutting between the two calico layers in the usual way. Turn the square round and you have your diamond–shaped decoration [113].

You could work several of these using the same thread, but with different lace filling stitches. Alternatively, you could incorporate beads into the decorations for added interest – just thread them onto the needle as you work.

Round Christmas tree decoration
This could be worked on a covered wire shape as in the diamond, but I have given different instructions here as this is a more usual method. You can also use the method described if you ever wish to put wire in with the cordonnette of a piece of lace – this is very useful for flowers and other three-dimensional lace.

Materials
- 28cm (11in) rustless wire for stiffening
- Medium thickness irridescent or metallic-effect thread
- Folded calico foundation backing
- Adhesive acetate film (to colour contrast with your chosen thread)
- Added ribbons, artificial flower and leaves for decoration if desired

Method
1 Trace the round design [114] onto plain paper. Cover it with adhesive film and tack it onto the calico foundation backing.

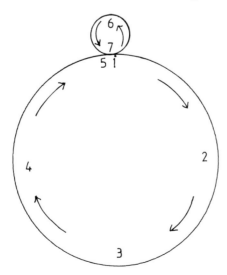

114 *Round decoration pattern. The numbers refer to the suggested direction of the figure-of-eight cordonnet couching.*

2 Couch the cordonnet around the outline, including the hanging ring. Follow the numbers on the design so that when you reach 5 you go into the loop in a figure-of-eight. You can commence your cordonnet anywhere, but you must remember both to interlock the starting loop of the cordonnet threads, and to whip the ends down firmly when you finish, just as if this were a normal piece of lace.

You can use the same irridescent or metallic-effect thread for your two couched cordonnet threads as you have chosen for the lace filling stitches. Alternatively you can use a matching crochet cotton or coton-à-broder thread of a similar thickness and colour instead.

3 Work the lace filling stitches within the circle, increasing and decreasing as necessary.

4 Using the same metallic or irridescent thread, buttonhole the cordonnette around the circle and hanging ring (the loops or 'knots' on the buttonhole stitches will face the outside as usual), incorporating the wire as described below. There is no need to lay in any threads when working this cordonnette unless you wish; you use the rustless wire instead, making sure that your buttonhole stitches are close enough to hide it.

A suitable starting point for your cordonnette would be on the main circle immediately below the hanging loop. If you are right-handed, work towards your left so that you can hold the single strand of wire in position with your left hand. Another method is to catch the wire down onto the cordonnet first with small whip stitches (on the surface) before you work the buttonholed cordonnette.

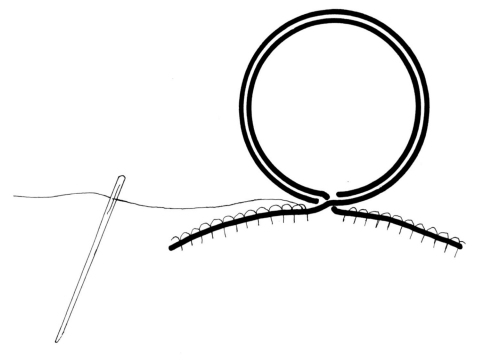

115 *Twisting the wire to make the cordonnette hanging loop.*

Leave about 2.5cm (1in) of wire before you start the buttonholing – this will prevent it from pulling out and can also be used to go around the hanging ring when you reach the end. Treat the wire just as you would any laid cordonnette threads in a normal piece of lace, laying it immediately over the cordonnet outline and buttonholing over both it and the original cordonnet. Work the cordonnette around the main circle until you come to the hanging loop, then just twist the end of the wire around to fit this loop. Do the same with the first 2.5cm (1in) of wire, so making a double thickness to the small loop here [115]. Cut off any excess wire and continue your buttonholing of the cordonnette around the hanging loop. End off your thread firmly.

5 Remove the completed decoration from the design and foundation by cutting between the calico layers as usual. Add any decorations such as ribbons or silk flowers if desired.

Cushion cover sampler

You can obviously work the cushion to other dimensions and colours to suit your own decor. The instructions given here are for a 38cm × 38cm (15in × 15in) cushion cover, which was worked in cream, gold and silver thread on an apple-green heavy silk fabric [116 and 117].

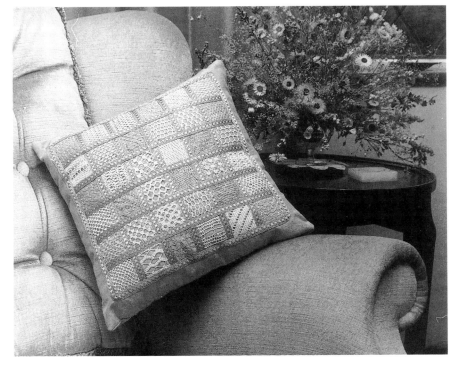

116 *Cushion-cover sampler.*

117 *Cushion-cover sampler (enlarged section).*

Materials (as used in the original)
- 2 skeins of cream number 16 coton-à-broder
- 1 reel silver DMC Fil Argent
- 1 reel gold DMC Fil Or à broder
- 2 pieces plain heavy furnishing silk or dupion-type material, each 43cm × 43cm (17in × 17in)
- 1 piece heavyweight iron-on stiffening (e.g. Vilene) 43cm × 43cm (17in × 17in)
- 4.5m (5yd) flat tape 1cm ($\frac{3}{8}$in) width
- 4.5m (5yd) decorative braid, 1cm ($\frac{3}{8}$in) width, or just over.

Method

The cushion cover front is made and used in a similar way to the calico sampler in Chapter 2. However, first iron on a heavy-weight stiffening to the back of the single piece of material so that it has more 'body' and is easier to work upon, since again you do not use adhesive acetate. The flat tape is covered by a decorative braid when you have completed all the fillings, and the cushion is then made up.

1 Iron the stiffening onto the back of one of the pieces of fabric. This will be the underside of the front of the cushion cover. The other piece is the back, which will not be used until the final making-up stage of the cushion.

2 Using tailor's chalk mark out a 30cm (12in) square exactly in the middle
   on the front of your stiffened cushion fabric piece. Divide this up into 5cm
   (2in) squares. This will give you 36 sampler areas and leave a border of
   6.5cm (2½in) all around.

3 These lines provide a guide for the flat plain tape. Leaving the outside
   edge lines until last, position lengths of tape centrally over the grid lines.
   Tack and machine the tape down the centre along these lines. In this way
   the edges of the tape in each area are left free.

   Finally, lay the tape in one piece around the outside of the square, again
   positioning it centrally over the lines, and machine it down the centre
   [118]. This will hold all the ends in place.

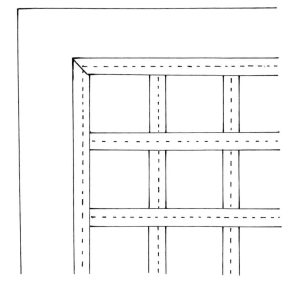

118 *Cushion sampler: laying the tapes.*

4 You are now ready to work your lace filling stitches with a ball-pointed
   needle in the sampler areas, just as you did for the practice sampler in
   Chapter 2. I started off with a knot at the back of the stiffened material and
   finished there with two or three back-stitches as well. As in the practice
   sampler, treat the tape edges of each square as your cordonnet.

   If you run out of ideas for every square, try repeating a stitch with a
   different tension or thread. If you use coloured threads, make sure that the
   finished effect is pleasingly colour balanced.

5 When all the sampler areas are filled, cover the plain tape with a
   decorative braid. Again leaving the outside edge until last, tack the braid
   down over the tapes and machine down both edges of the braid so that it
   is flat [119]. Tack and machine a length of braid over the edge tape,
   making sure that you have neat corners and that the end is tucked under
   and so does not fray.

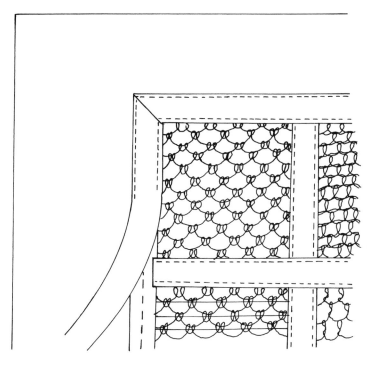

119 *Cushion sampler: stitching on the decorative braid.*

6 Make up your cushion cover, using the other piece of fabric for the back. Machine both pieces together (right sides facing) allowing a 2.5cm (1in) seam. Leave an opening at the lower edge for the cushion pad or filling. Turn right side out, insert the cushion pad and catch stitch the opening carefully together.

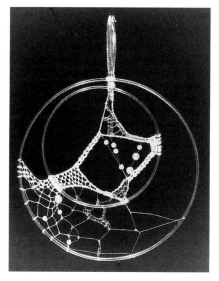

120 *Modern experimental needlepoint lace hanging worked in cream and gold, (inspired by work on a single ring in 'Naaldkant Speels en Luchtig'). (Photograph reduced from original size.)*

five
Decorative finishes

The beautiful Venetian raised laces, such as the heavily padded Venetian gros point (frontispiece) and rose point, illustrate the superb effect given by the use of decorative and padded cordonnettes and added couronnes. This chapter gives basic methods for working a wide selection of decorative finishes. The leaf motif project at the end of the chapter incorporates some of these to make a very effective small piece of lace.

For clarity, the buttonhole stitches of the cordonnette are shown spaced in the diagrams. **When you work your lace they should be touching**.

Looped or scalloped cordonnettes

A pretty scalloped edge can be given to the cordonnette as you are working it. The inserted daisy motif in Chapter 3 was worked with a simple scalloped cordonnette around the central circle. The Venetian-style leaf motif at the end of this chapter [121] also has a scalloped edge, but with the addition of long Venetian picots to each small scallop.

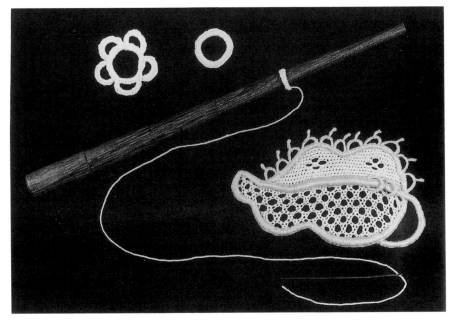

121 *The Venetian Gros Point style leaf motif, together with a ring stick and couronne rings.*

Simple scalloped cordonnette

Plan out, or estimate, the number of scallops required along your design so that they are of equal size. Strictly speaking, there should be the same number of stitches in the cordonnette of the straight part of each scallop.

Commencing your cordonnette over the laid threads in the usual manner, work the cordonnette buttonhole stitches along the edge just for the required length of the straight base part of one scallop.

Go back to the edge 'loop' of the first stitch and pass the needle and thread through it [122], making sure your last stitch remains tight.

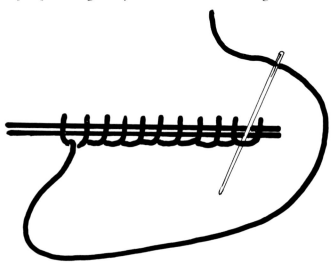

122 *Simple scalloped cordonnette: commencing the scallop foundation threads.*

Keeping this thread in a small loop the required size of your scallop, pass the needle and thread through the edge loop of your last cordonnette buttonhole stitch [123], thus making a second thread to the scallop.

Form the third thread of the scallop foundation by repeating the step for making your first foundation thread. You now have a foundation of three

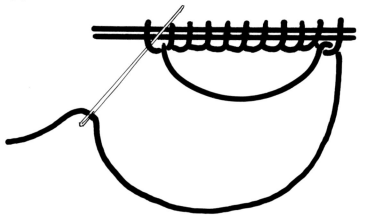

123 *Simple scalloped cordonnette: making the second foundation thread.*

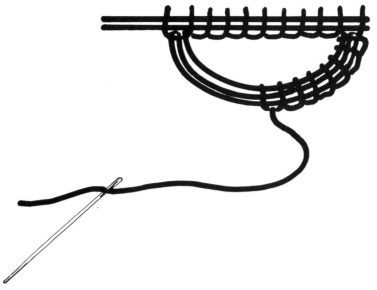

124 *Simple scalloped cordonnette: buttonholing over the three foundation threads.*

threads over which you buttonhole to make the scallop. The buttonhole 'loops' should lie towards the outside [124]. Work your stitches closely along the whole scallop loop.

Work your cordonnette stitches along the edge to form the straight part of the next scallop, working one additional stitch. I like to have one stitch between each scallop loop so that they lie well.

Form your three scallop foundation threads as before, leaving one stitch between the scallops [125], and buttonhole the scallop. Continue working your scallops in this manner.

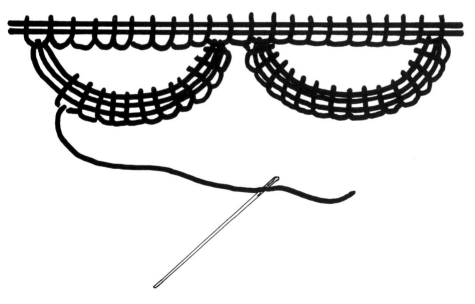

125 *Working the next scallop.*

97

Double layer scalloped cordonnette

This pretty edge is found in several of the old Venetian laces, and consists of groups of paired scallops, each with a third scallop. The method of working is very similar to the simple scalloped edge.

Work one complete scallop and then form the three foundation threads of the second scallop. Work the buttonhole stitches only halfway along this scallop.

Form the first of the three foundation threads for the third scallop, from here to the centre top of the first scallop, by passing the needle and thread through the edge loop of the central stitch [126]. Then form the other two threads.

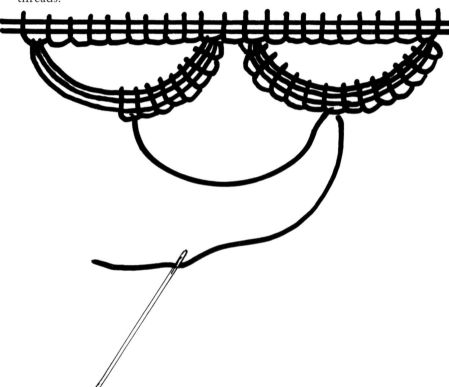

126 *Double layer scalloped cordonnette: forming the foundation for the third scallop.*

Buttonhole along this third scallop, and continue the buttonholing of the remaining half of the second scallop. Continue making groups of scallops in this way, remembering to leave one stitch between each of the scallops along the straight edge.

Using these basic instructions, further variations can be worked. You can also incorporate simple picots and Venetian picots. Instructions for these are given overleaf.

Useful hint

Should you wish to add scallops to an already buttonholed
cordonnette, or have forgotten to incorporate them, the following
emergency method is very useful:

1 Instead of working over three foundation threads each time, only
  two are formed so that you can make a progressive line of scallops.
  Join on your thread to the worked cordonnette at the start of your
  first desired scallop. Make the first foundation thread by passing the
  needle and thread through the edge loop of the cordonnette where
  you wish your scallop to end.

2 Make the second foundation thread as usual and buttonhole over
  these two threads so forming the scallop [127].

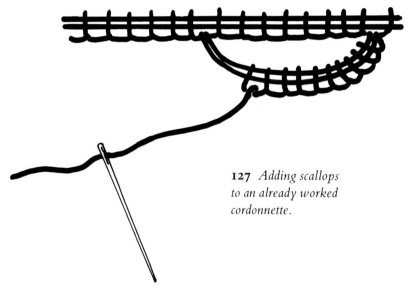

127 *Adding scallops
to an already worked
cordonnette.*

3 You will now be ready to make the next scallop, forming and
  working over two foundation threads. You can either work one
  simple buttonhole stitch into the cordonnette between each of your
  scallops, or work them directly next to each other.

Picots

These give added interest to the decorative finishes on lace. They may
be worked on the cordonnette as here, on bars linking motifs together
(see chapter 6), or even to embellish couronne rings and loops.

Simple loop picot

Working your cordonnette, buttonhole from the right to the left until you reach the position of the desired picot. Stick a pin into the pillow through the work at the point where you wish the loop to reach. (If you are not working on a pillow, pass the point up again through your design and foundation.) This gives the length of your picot. It can be varied as desired, but 3mm ($\frac{1}{8}$in) is an average size for practice.

Take the thread to the left behind the pin and down towards you behind the edge and the laid cordonnette threads at the left of the pin [128], so forming a loop caught by the pin.

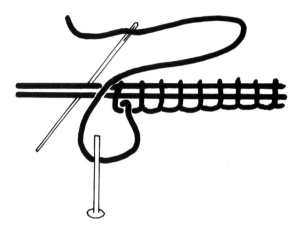

128 *Simple loop picot: loop caught by the pin.*

Holding the thread with the thumb of your left hand, take it down to the left and back over to the right as in the diagram. Pass the needle under both threads of the loop held by the pin, and under the right-hand thread of the loop held by your thumb, then over the left thread [129].

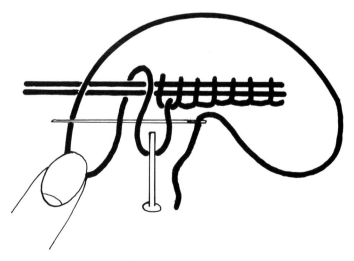

129 *Simple loop picot: making the 'knotted' picot loop.*

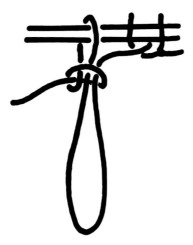

Take your thumb off the work and firmly pull up this 'knot' holding the picot loop which is still around the pin. Remove the pin and continue the cordonnette [130].

Picots can be worked successively with only a stitch between each, or spaced out further as desired. The length is dictated by the position of the pin.

Venetian picot

These are a feature of the old Venetian raised laces and are more elaborate than the simple picot. Similar, but not identical, picots were also worked in many of the old French needlepoint laces, such as Alençon.

In modern work they are excellent for creating thorns on lace roses, and also for giving added interest to scallops. The Venetian-style leaf motif project shows simple scallops, each with a long Venetian picot.

Working your cordonnette (or scallop or bar) buttonhole from the right to the left until you reach the position of the desired Venetian picot. Stick a

131 *Venetian picot: buttonhole stitch around pin.*

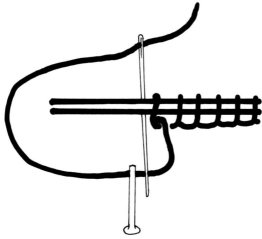

101

pin into the pillow (as you did with the simple picot) at the point where you want the end of the picot to be. In old laces they were often only about 1mm long. **It helps to think of your Venetian picot in two stages – making a buttonhole stitch incorporating the pin, and then buttonholing along this.**

Take the thread behind the pin to the left and work a buttonhole cordonnette stitch [131], bringing the needle out to the right of the pin.

Again, take the thread behind the pin to the left and loop it over to the right. Pass the needle over the right thread of the buttonhole stitch which is around the pin, under both the right thread of this new loop and under the left thread of the buttonhole stitch, then lastly over the left-hand thread of the new loop [132]. Take the needle through and pull up. Effectively, you have made a 'knot' at the end of your buttonhole loop, which will stop the next buttonhole stitches from falling off the end of the picot!

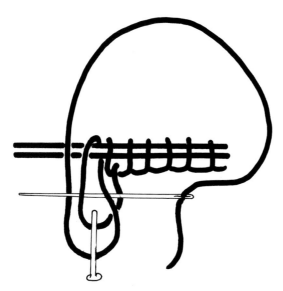

132 *Venetian picot: making the holding 'knot' before buttonholing up the picot.*

Buttonhole closely back up this foundation to the cordonnette, still keeping the pin in place as this holds the picot in position. Your needle will now be passing under all the foundation threads. Then remove the pin and continue your cordonnette buttonholing until you wish to make another picot.

If you are working a Venetian picot on a scallop it is advisable to keep the pin in place after working the picot until the scallop is completely buttonholed.

Raised (padded) cordonnette

The cordonnette can be padded or raised as you are buttonholing it. It is this padding which gave the old raised Venetian laces their almost 'sculptured' look.

A similar method can be used today to give a very interesting extra dimension and 'finish' to your lace. It is particularly effective if you graduate the amount of padding, especially on the curves of a design, as in the leaf motif in this chapter.

If you are right-handed it is best to work your buttonholing from right to left (so that the 'loops' of the buttonhole stitches are towards you). In this way, you can hold the extra laid padding threads in position with your left hand. If you are left-handed, work towards the right.

I like to use either a crochet cotton Number 20, or coton-à-broder Number 16 for the padding threads of raised work, even though the lace filling stitches and cordonnette buttonholing are worked in another generally much finer thread. When working in colour try to use a similar colour padding thread so that any gaps in your buttonholing do not show.

Commence and work your cordonnette as usual, buttonholing closely over the normal two laid threads (see Chapter 2), until you are at the position where you wish to start increasing and padding the cordonnette.

Using about 15cm (6in) of the padding thread doubled over, place the ends of this folded thread to the inner side of the cordonnette so that your buttonhole stitches will now catch this in as well [133]. Leave a 'tail' of 1cm ($\frac{3}{8}$in) of each cut end sticking out. The padding threads can be laid in singly, but I like to use a doubled thread like this.

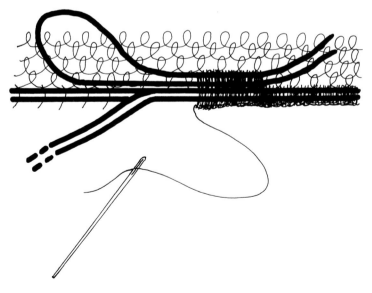

133 *Raised (padded) cordonnette: laying in a doubled-over padding thread.*

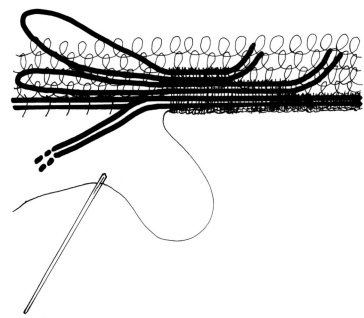

Continue the cordonnette buttonholing for about 2mm ($\frac{1}{12}$in), enclosing the two padding threads as well. Then lay in another doubled thread, again to the inner side, so that your buttonholing now includes these in the cordonnette. Leave 'tails' as before [134].

Continue the cordonnette buttonholing for another 2mm ($\frac{1}{12}$in), enclosing these new padding threads as well. You can now draw up the 'tails' of the first padding threads so that they disappear. Never just cut them off; they will show. **Make sure you avoid whiskery tails on the padding threads. The ends should be cleanly cut so that they will disappear completely when pulled through.**

It is advisable to work at least 4mm ($\frac{1}{6}$in) of cordonnette over any padding thread before you draw up the tails, since this holds the threads in place. Draw up one thread of the pair by gently pulling it through from the folded end, until the tail disappears under the worked cordonnette. Then gently pull up the other thread of this pair until its tail disappears. Be warned, sooner or later we all find that we have pulled a thread out completely, so pull them through gently!

Continue your cordonnette buttonholing, laying in new padding threads and drawing up the tails until the desired thickness is obtained. You will find that you need to add quite a few pairs of padding threads. **If you are not sure which thread at the fold should be pulled to draw up a 'tail', just pull this tail end and you will see the corresponding length move near the fold.**

When your cordonnette has reached your chosen maximum thickness, usually at the apex of a curve, you then need to decrease the padding. This is easier than adding in, since you just cut off pairs of threads in stages. I prefer to choose the two threads from underneath each time, if possible. This makes the decrease smoother and leaves the two long original laid cordonnette threads uncut, thus keeping a strong outline. Lift up the bundle of padding threads and cut off the two chosen threads closely. Continue with your cordonnette buttonholing, cutting off the threads in stages to correspond with the increasing on the other side of the curve.

There are other methods of 'raising' or padding the cordonnette; this is the one I use most often.

Branches

Branches are worked in a similar manner to an ordinary cordonnette, by branching some of the threads off when the branch is reached.

When you reach the branch, lay out on this side the desired number of threads. This will depend mainly on the required thickness of the side branch [135]. The cordonnette buttonholing of the branch will be worked later.

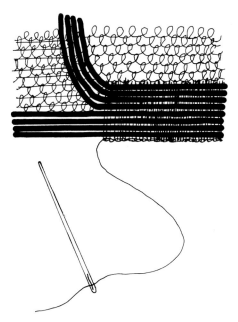

135 *Branches in a padded cordonnette.*

Since the main cordonnette padding now has fewer threads, lay in the required make-up number at this point before going on with the buttonholing of the main cordonnette. Should you be decreasing near a branch, you can, of course, use the branch threads to help reduce the outline.

Difficulties are sometimes encountered when your padded cordonnette has to pass over an already buttonholed and padded cordonnette. The

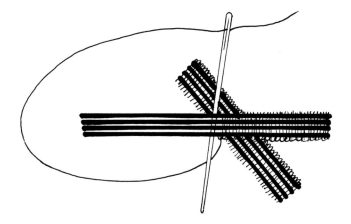

simplest way is to work the new cordonnette almost like a bridge over the other one. In this case, buttonhole only around the surface laid threads and padding threads. The needle just passes under these laid threads, it does not go right under the original outline and worked cordonnette [136]. This is only necessary for a few stitches, at the point where the cordonnettes cross.

Ending off
A padded cordonnette is ended off like an ordinary cordonnette. (See Chapter 2.) The only difference is that you reduce the number of padding threads just before you end off your cordonnette.

To help prevent unwanted gaps appearing between the buttonhole stitches of a padded cordonnette, make sure that you work them very closely. I find also, that occasionally lifting up the laid threads and gently pulling them towards the worked cordonnette stitches seems to 'wedge' them together more.

Couronnes

Couronnes are the final decorations added to a piece of lace. They are often made separately and stitched in place once the lace is finished and has been removed from the calico foundation.

The simplest are couronne rings [121], made on a ring-stick, dowel, or even a knitting needle. They can be used to add interest at the centre of flowers, either singly with or without scallops, or perhaps in different sizes to give a 'stepped' centre.

Simple couronne ring
This is really only a circle of foundation threads covered with simple

buttonhole stitches. It is made in the hand as it is not necessary to couch down the outline.

Start by trying to make a simple ring on a piece of wooden dowel rod 1cm (⅜in) in diameter. Alternatively, use a knitting needle of a similar size. Crochet cotton Number 40 is a good choice for this practice ring. In an actual piece of lace, you would use the same thread as your lace filling stitches or cordonnette buttonholing.

Using a slightly longer than normal length of crochet cotton, or other thread, wind the end firmly, but not too tightly, three or four times around the dowel. The direction of winding does not really matter. However, I find that, being right-handed, I like to wind it anti-clockwise so that I can then make my buttonhole stitches downwards towards me in an anti-clockwise direction. They can also be worked away from you. In this case, my left hand then holds the end in position.

Still holding the foundation ring on the dowel, work two or three buttonhole stitches. The needle passes under all the threads each time [137]. The 'knots' or loops should be on the outer edge.

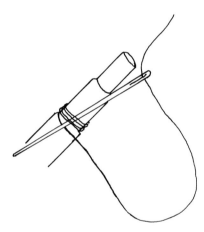

137 *Beginning a couronne ring on a ring-stick.*

Continue to buttonhole completely around the ring, either keeping it on the dowel, or just holding it between your finger and thumb. The end is worked in as you go.

Finally, take the needle and thread through the 'loop' of your first stitch to join the ring of stitches. End off by making one buttonhole stitch, running the needle and thread a short way under the stitches and then cutting off the thread. If you want, you can leave a short length of thread which can be used later to stitch the ring to your finished lace, once it has been removed from the calico foundation.

This is a basic method for making a simple couronne ring. The thickness can be altered by winding on more turns of thread when making the foundation ring. If you are making several, then remember to keep the number of foundation threads the same. The diameter can be changed by using different size dowel or knitting needles. Special wooden ring-sticks can be bought which have stepped sizes of diameter.

If you wish to make couronne rings to fit a specific size circle in your lace, there is a simple way to find the correct size of dowel, or area on your ring-stick. Just lay the stick over the circle, until you can see a smallish gap each side, thus allowing for the space taken up by the foundation threads and buttonhole stitches.

Couronne ring with scallops
This ring is worked in a similar manner to the simple ring; the scallops are worked as you make the buttonhole stitches, using the method for working the scalloped cordonnette at the beginning of this chapter.

As before, make the foundation circle of threads around the dowel, or ring-stick first. Estimate the number of scallops required on your couronne ring, so that you know how many stitches are worked along the base part of each scallop section. You can then work your scallops as you buttonhole around the foundation circle [138].

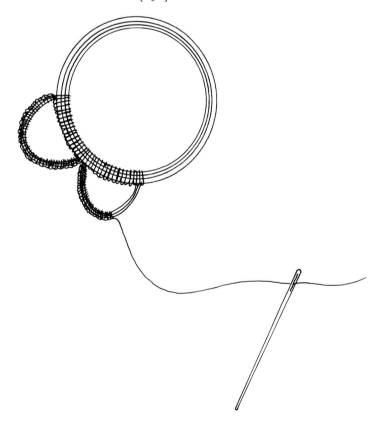

138 *Couronne ring with scallops.*

'Disappearing' couronne rings

These very effective couronne rings are worked onto an existing worked cordonnette; for example, the mid-rib of the leaf brooch [121], so that the rings look as if they are threaded onto the padded cordonnette. They are generally worked in the same thread as the buttonholing of the cordonnette, and were first shown to me by Catherine Barley.

First, lay the small tip of the ring-stick (or medium size knitting needle) on the worked cordonnette. Thread a ball-pointed needle with a length of the thread which was used for the buttonhole stitches of this cordonnette. Passing the needle tip right under the cordonnette each time, make your foundation circle of three or more turns around the tip of the ring-stick and cordonnette [139].

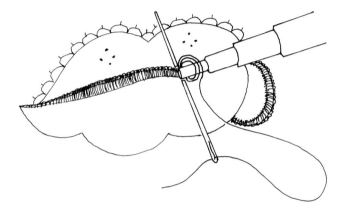

139 *'Disappearing' couronne ring.*

Keeping the ring-stick in position all or part of the time, work the buttonhole stitches over the visible part of the foundation circle. Since the 'disappearing' ring might move about slightly, work your stitches close together, going right up to the cordonnette both where the ring appears and disappears. Picots can also be worked on this ring. End off by running the thread under the worked cordonnette below.

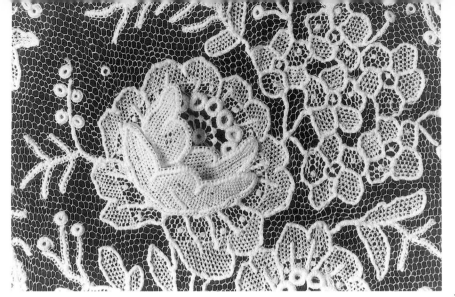

140 *Portion of Point de Gaze collar [71] enlarged to show a chain of couronne rings in the centre of the large flowers.*

Chain of rings

When unpicking some tiny scraps of old Point de Gaze lace, I was fascinated to see different methods of working a series of rings. The lace filling stitches had all been worked as had the cordonnette except where the rings were to be worked [140].

In the first method, the laid threads for this part of the cordonnette were laid down in place as a series of loops [141]. These loops were then

141 *Chain of rings (1).*

buttonholed to make a series of circles so that the tiny lengths of laid threads between each disappeared.

In the second method, the laid cordonnette threads were placed down as two 'waves' [142], which were then buttonholed into circles.

142 *Chain of rings (2).*

In the third method, the laid cordonnette threads were placed down again as two waves [143], which were then buttonholed into circles.

143 *Chain of rings (3).*

These three methods could all be used to make lines or circles of small rings, instead of ordinary single couronne rings which are stab-stitched down afterwards.

Project

Leaf motif in Venetian Gros Point style

Some of the decorative finishes at the beginning of this chapter can be used in working this leaf motif. The leaf may be worn as a brooch if a brooch-pin is stitched to the back. It can also be combined with the daisy motif from Chapter 3 to make up a variety of designs.

The thread used in the old Venetian raised laces was extremely fine – often there were more than 6,000 stitches in a square inch!

The leaf illustrated [121] was worked in pale cream 100/3 Gutterman silk, with a darker cream cordonnette also in 100/3 silk.

Materials
- Number 20 crochet cotton for the cordonnet outline and the laid and padding threads of the cordonnette (preferably to colour match the lace thread).
- Matching sewing cotton for the cordonnet couching.
- Fine thread for the lace filling stitches, the cordonnette buttonholing and any couronnes, (for example, 100/3 twisted silk thread or other fine thread).
- Foundation calico.
- Adhesive acetate.
- Brooch pin (optional).

Note: If you think the suggested threads will be too fine for you, then use a thicker thread such as 40/3 twisted silk for the lace fillings, but try to work the cordonnette buttonholing in the fine thread.

Method
Refer back to other chapters if necessary. The outline instructions here assume that you have already worked a simple piece of lace, such as the daisy motif. Use the picture [121] of the finished leaf as a guide. The stitches used are typical Venetian ones and its design incorporates further aspects of working needlepoint lace.
1 Using the leaf motif [144], couch down the cordonnet outline of Number 20 crochet cotton as usual. Commence the cordonnet at 1 and follow the numbers. (Your motif will be upside-down as you start the couching of the stalk). When you have passed 6, remember to interlock the starting loop at 1 and you can also pass the laid threads between the two that have

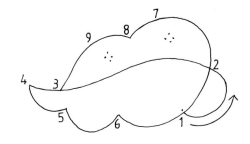

144 *Leaf motif: Venetian Gros Point style.*

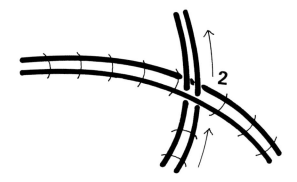

145 *Leaf motif: the cordonnet junction at 2 is interlocked when couching from 6 to 7.*

already been couched at 2 [145]. End off your cordonnet as usual when you have passed 9 and reach 3 again.

2 Start at the upper edge of the leaf, using the fine thread, and work the lace filling in the top half of the leaf in corded stitch, incorporating the two four-hole diamonds. Work the stitches so that they are parallel to the vein along the centre of the leaf. This will present you with the problem of how to work the two curves at the top!

Start your first row near 9 on the diagram and work in cloth stitch until the top of the left curve is complete and you have worked your stitch row ending at 8. Run the working thread under the cordonnet couching stitches to 7 and then work the first row here across to the right [146].

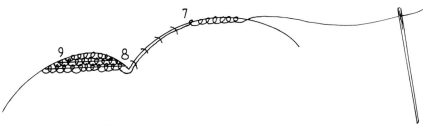

146 *Leaf motif: method for working the two curves.*

Complete the filling in this top right curve until the last stitch row is level with 8. The two curves are now complete. Next, take the 'cord' right across to the left side, so that your subsequent row of stitches goes across the whole shape [147]. Continue the filling as usual.

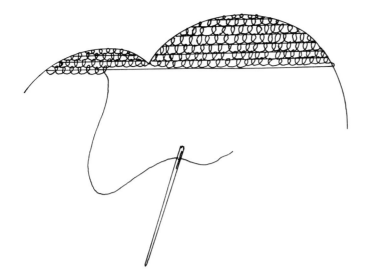

If you are left-handed and prefer to work from the right, start on the
right at the top of the right curve and work in a similar way to the
previous instructions. When both curves are complete, your cord will be
laid right across from left to right below 8. This method can be used to
work any uneven shapes such as this.

3 Work the lace filling in the lower half of the leaf in pea stitch variation.
Your first row will go right across the area from 4 to 2. Complete this
half, decreasing and increasing as necessary.

4 Work the cordonnette – this is buttonholed in the fine thread over
Number 20 crochet cotton laid threads.

If you are right-handed, turn your lace upside-down and start your
cordonnette where the cordonnet outline ended at 3, working your
cordonnette towards 9. In this way you are working to the left, and you
can hold the laid cordonnette threads in place with your left-hand.

If you are left-handed, I suggest you still start at 3 and work towards 9,
but keep your lace the right way up. In this way, you will be working
your cordonnette buttonhole stitches away from you, but you will be able
to hold the laid threads in place with your right hand.

The cordonnette of the leaf is designed so that it is worked in one
continuous flow. It is worked over two laid cordonnette threads (in this
case, of Number 20 crochet cotton). The buttonholing is in the fine
thread. Padding threads are added where required, using Number 20
crochet cotton. You will actually work the cordonnette in this motif in
the opposite direction to the laying of the original cordonnet outline, so
ending at 1.

Work a scalloped cordonnette, with slightly longer than usual Venetian picots on each scallop, along the upper edge of the leaf. Continue the cordonnette from 7 past 2 towards 6 along the lower edge of the leaf, adding and removing padding threads as necessary to give the curves. Reduce the padding as you work around the tip of the leaf. The mid-vein and stalk are worked last.

Continue the cordonnette from 4 to 3 and work along the mid-vein which is again padded. At 2 it will pass over the already-worked cordonnette and continue as the stalk, ending at 1. Reduce the padding slightly here and end off in the normal way.

5 Work two disappearing couronne rings around the padded vein cordonnette, again in the fine thread.

6 Remove the completed lace from the covered design and foundation in the usual way, tidying up any couching threads which are still attached. You will find that tweezers are useful for this. If you wish to make it into a brooch, stitch the brooch-pin to the underside of the vein of the leaf.

six

Design, colour and threads

Design

Once you have learnt the basic techniques of needlepoint lace, it is exciting to make up your own designs. Having made lace yourself, you now have an idea of what will work and what will not, and also the knowledge to carry out your designs.

There are several good books available from which you can learn about design techniques and colour theory. Inspiration for design comes from many sources – scenery, art galleries and museums, old lace, fabrics and magazine pictures, to name but a few. Ideas may come from other crafts. Indeed often in the past, a style or 'movement' in one art or craft influenced many others. If you really feel that you cannot design yourself, then look for ideas from embroidery and children's colouring books, as well as lace books. You might also find it helpful to keep a small notebook or file of ideas for future use. The abstract sketch illustrated [148] is such an example.

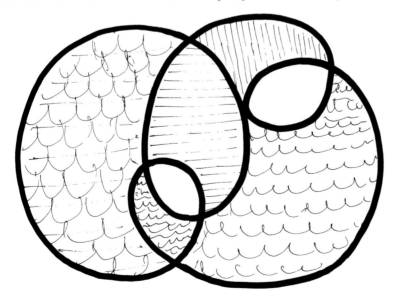

148 *Preliminary abstract sketch for a design.*

Everyone has their own way of designing, but the following ideas may be of help to you.

When planning out designs for my own lace I generally use a soft 3B pencil or black felt-tip pen to sketch the ideas, since these give a pleasing flowing line. Do not worry too much about erasing in these preliminary sketches. If you turn your design upside-down and it still looks balanced, then it is probably a good design.

Designs can be enlarged or reduced [149 and 150]. Many photocopiers can do this for you easily.

149 *Small mat design (suitable for medium-fine threads; adapted from a design in Min-ju Sun's Oriental Floral Designs . . . See Further reading).*
Key – The fine lines show the position of the buttonholed bars, the dotted lines the position of rows of twisted single Bruxelles in the cloth stitch areas.
C = corded stitch.

When you have a final design, it is extremely helpful to shade in the areas which will be worked. This gives a good idea of the final effect and the balance between the worked and open areas – illustration 152 shows this shading-in of the small mat design from this chapter.

Colour and design

If I am using colour in my lace I paint in the colours on a copy of the design to get a good balance. Especially when working in colour I also limit the number of types of stitch used, otherwise the lace may look too 'busy'.

150 *Enlarged mat design (suitable for medium-thick threads, with bars in finer thread).*

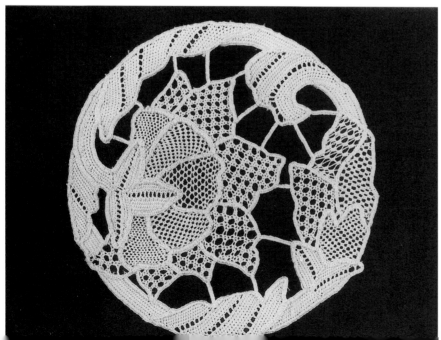

151 *The small mat (worked by Irene Day) using DMC cordonnet 80 thread.*

152 *Small mat design shaded to show the balance of the worked and open areas.*

The best stitch to give depth and 'body' to any design is probably close corded single Bruxelles stitch. The lovely Irish Youghal lace illustrated [153] uses this stitch to perfection, showing the contrast it gives to the more lacy stitches. This stitch also gives stability to your lace and so is ideal for use near the edges of designs, such as in the lace mat [151], where the choice of the other stitches is your own.

153 *Irish Youghal lace (mid-nineteenth century) belonging to the author.*

Bars

Areas of lace may be joined by 'bars' which are generally buttonholed. The bars are worked before your cordonnette buttonholing. Simple bars may be worked as follows:

1 Using the same thread as you would use for your cordonnette buttonhole stitches, or an even finer one, take it two or three times across and under the two cordonnet edges [154], thus making the foundation threads for the bar.

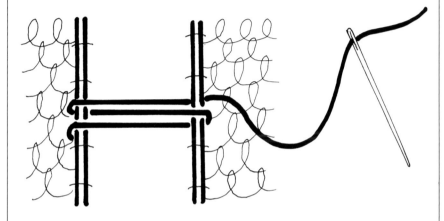

154 *Buttonholed bar: making the foundation threads of the bar.*

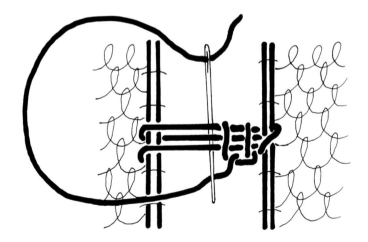

155 *Buttonholed bar: buttonholing over the threads (In the actual work the stitches would be closely next to each other).*

2 Buttonhole across this bar [155], and whip along the cordonnet to the position of the next bar. Bars may also be decorated with loops and picots which are worked as you buttonhole the bar.

The choice of colour in lace is very personal, some people prefer to use white or cream, others like to develop and extend their work by means of colour and variety of thread. Although I enjoy the classical clear-cut effect of pure white lace, I like working in soft muted colours as well, since I find it almost like painting.

Threads

You could also try working a modern lace design in white, or cream, or one colour, using a variety of types and thicknesses of thread. A sampler is useful here so that you can see the effect of a chosen thread.

However, remember that for a more traditional piece of lace the thickness of thread is important in relation to the size of the design. Generally, the smaller the design, the finer the thread, although in past centuries large areas were all worked in very fine thread. You may also prefer to work large areas in fine thread.

Mounting

If you wish to mount your lace after working, choose the colour of the backing carefully, as it should enhance the lace and is all part of designing.

156 *Evening bag with applied Venetian Gros Point style needlepoint lace, worked in shades of pink 100/3 silks.*

157 *Design for Venetian Gros Point style motif in illus. 156. Worked in shades of pink 100/3 silk and appliquéd onto a pink silk evening bag.*
Key –
C = corded stitch.
~ – – = twisted stitch row,
P.V = Pea stitch variation,
= looped cordonnette with Venetian picots,
= padded cordonnette.

White lace is effective on black or blue, and cream lace looks good on brown or green. Choosing a backing is especially important if you use colours in your work – the background colour will either lift and enhance the lace or kill it!

I find the best way is actually to lay the completed lace (off its calico foundation and design) on various coloured background materials to see the effect. Quite often the backing looks best if it is in the same colour as one of the main thread colours.

For me, one of the joys of needlepoint lace is its flexibility. It gives the lace maker so much scope in both design and application, whether quite simple or more ambitious. Once you have learnt the basic techniques of this lovely lace the possibilities are almost endless!

Suppliers

England

BEDFORDSHIRE
Mrs Sells
Lane Cove
49 Pedley Lane
Clifton
Shefford SG17 5QT

BERKSHIRE
Chrisken Bobbins
26 Cedar Drive
Kingsclere RG15 8TD

BUCKINGHAMSHIRE
J. S. Sear
Lacecraft Supplies
8 Hillview
Sherington MK16 9NJ

Winslow Bobbins
70 Magpie Way
Winslow MK18 3PZ

SMP
4 Garners Close
Chalfont St Peter SL9 0HB

CAMBRIDGESHIRE
Josie and Jeff Harrison
Walnut Cottage
Winwick
Huntingdon PE17 5PP

Heffers Graphic Shop
(*matt coloured transparent
adhesive film*)
26 King Street
Cambridge CB1 1LN

Spangles
Carole Morris
Cashburn Lane
Burwell CB5 0ED

CHESHIRE
Lynn Turner
Church Meadow Crafts
7 Woodford Lane
Winsford CW7 1LN

DEVON
Honiton Lace Shop
44 High Street
Honiton EX14 8PJ

DORSET
F. Herring & Sons
27 High West Street
Dorchester DT1 1UP

T. Parker (*mail order,
general and bobbins*)
124 Corhampton Road
Boscombe East
Bournemouth BH6 5NZ

ESSEX
Needlework courses
Anne Bartlett
Bucklers Farm
Coggeshall CO6 1SB

GLOUCESTERSHIRE
T. Brown (*bobbins*)
Temple Lane Cottage
Littledean
Cinderford

Chosen Crafts Centre
46 Winchcombe Street
Cheltenham GL52 2ND

HAMPSHIRE
Needlestyle
24–26 West Street
Alresford SO24 9AT

Richard Viney (*bobbins*)
Unit 7
Port Royal Street
Southsea PO5 3UD

ISLE OF WIGHT
Busy Bobbins
Unit 7
Scarrots Lane
Newport
PO30 1JD

KENT
The Handicraft Shop
47 Northgate
Canterbury CT1 1BE

Denis Hornsby
25 Manwood Avenue
Canterbury CT2 7AH

Francis Iles
73 High Street
Rochester ME1 1LX

LANCASHIRE
Malcolm J. Fielding (*bobbins*)
2 Northern Terrace
Moss Lane
Silverdale LA5 0ST

LINCOLNSHIRE
Ken and Pat Schultz
Whynacres
Shepeau Stow
Whaplode Drove
Spalding PE12 0TU

MERSEYSIDE
Hayes & Finch
Head Office & Factory
Hanson Road
Aintree
Liverpool L9 9BP

MIDDLESEX
Redburn Crafts
Squires Garden Centre
Halliford Road
Upper Halliford
Shepperton TW17 8RU

NORFOLK
Stitches and Lace
(*mail order*)
Alby Craft Centre
Cromer Road
Alby
Norwich NR11 7QE

Jane's Pincushions
Taverham Craft Unit 4
Taverham Nursery Centre
Fir Covert Road
Taverham
Norwich NR8 6HT

George Walker
The Corner Shop
Rickinghall
Diss

NORTH HUMBERSIDE
Teazle Embroideries
35 Boothferry Road
Hull

NORTH YORKSHIRE
The Craft House
23 Bar Street
Scarborough YO11 2HT

Stitchery
Finkle Street
Richmond

SOUTH YORKSHIRE
D. H. Shaw
47 Lamor Crescent
Thrushcroft
Rotherham S66 9QD

STAFFORDSHIRE
J. & J. Ford (*mail order
and lace days only*)
October Hill
65 Upper Way
Upper Longdon
Rugeley
WS16 1QB

SUFFOLK
A. R. Archer (*bobbins*)
The Poplars
Shetland
near Stowmarket IP14 3DE

Mary Collins (*linen by the
metre, and made up
articles of church linen*)
Church Furnishings
St Andrews Hall
Humber Doucy Lane
Ipswich IP4 3BP

E. & J. Piper (*silk
embroidery and lace
thread*)
Silverlea
Flax Lane
Glemsford CO10 7RS

SURREY
Needle and Thread
80 High Street
Horsell
Woking GU21 4SZ

Needlestyle
5 The Woolmead
Farnham GU9 7TX

SUSSEX
Southern Handicrafts
20 Kensington Gardens
Brighton BN1 4AC

WARWICKSHIRE
Christine & David Springett
21 Hillmorton Road
Rugby CV22 5DF

WEST MIDLANDS
Framecraft
83 Hamstead Road
Handsworth Wood
Birmingham B2 1JA

The Needlewoman
21 Needles Alley
off New Street
Birmingham B2 5AE

Stiches
Dovehouse Shopping Parade
Warwick Road
Olton, Solihull

WEST YORKSHIRE
Jo Firth
Lace Marketing &
   Needlecraft Supplies
58 Kent Crescent
Lowtown
Pudsey LS28 9EB

Just Lace
Lacemaker Supplies
14 Ashwood Gardens
Gildersome
Leeds LS27 7AS

Sebalace
Waterloo Mills
Howden Road
Silsden BD20 0AH

George White Lacemaking
   Supplies
40 Heath Drve
Boston Spa LS23 6PB

WILTSHIRE
Doreen Campbell (*frames
and mounts*)
Highcliff
Bremilham Road
Malmesbury SN16 0DQ

Scotland
Christine Riley
53 Barclay Street
Stonehaven
Kincardineshire

Peter & Beverley Scarlet
Strupak
Hill Head
Cold Wells, Ellon
Grampian

Wales
Bryncraft Bobbins
B. J. Phillips
Pantaglas
Cellan
Lampeter
Dyfed SA48 8JD

Hilkar Lace Suppliers
33 Mysydd Road
Landore
Swansea

Australia
Australian Lace magazine
P.O. Box 609
Manly
NSW 2095

Dentelles Lace Supplies
c/o Betty Franks
39 Lang Terrace
Northgate 4013
Brisbane
Queensland

The Lacemaker
724a Riversdale Road
Camberwell
Victoria 3124

Spindle and Loom
Arcade 83
Longueville Road
Lane Cove
NSW 2066

Tulis Crafts
201 Avoca Street
Randwick
NSW 2031

Belgium
't Handwerkhuisje
Katelijnestraat 23
8000 Bruges

Kantcentrum
Balstraat 14
8000 Bruges

Manufacture Belge de
   Dentelle
6 Galerie de la Reine
Galeries Royales St
   Hubert
1000 Bruxelles

Orchidée
Mariastraat 18
8000 Bruges

Ann Thys
't Apostelientje
Balstraat 11
8000 Bruges

France
Centre d'Enseignement à
   la Dentelle du Puy
2 Rue Duguesclin
43000 Le Puy en Velay

A l'Econome
Anne-Marie Deydier
Ecole de Dentelle aux
   Fuseaux
10 rue Paul Chenavard
69001 Lyon

Rougier and Plé
13–15 bd des Filles de
   Calvaire
75003 Paris

Germany
Barbara Fay
Verlag &
   Versandbuchhandlung
Am Goosberg 2
D-W 2330 Gammelby

P. P. Hempel
Ortolanweg 34
1000 Berlin 47

Holland
Blokker's Boektiek
Bronsteeweg 4/4a
2101 AC Heemstede

Theo Brejaart
Dordtselaan 146–148
P.O. Box 5199
3008 AD Rotterdam

Heikina de Rüyter
Zuiderstraat 1
9693 ER Nieweschans

Magazijn *De Vlijt*
Lij nmarkt 48
Utrecht

Netherlands
Tiny van Donschor
Postbus 482
6000 A1 Weert

Switzerland
Buchhandlung
Dr A. Scheidegger & Co.
   AG
Obere Bahnhofstr. 10A
CH-8901 Affoltern a.A.

Martin Burkhard
Klöppelzubehör
Jurastrasse 7
CH-5300 Turgi

Fadehax
Inh. Irene Solca
4105 Biel-Benken
Basel

New Zealand
Peter McLeavey
P.O. Box 69.007
Auckland 8

USA
Arbor House
22 Arbor Lane
Roslyn Heights
NY 11577

Baltazor Inc.
3262 Severn Avenue
Metairie
LA 7002

Beggars' Lace
P.O. Box 481223
Denver
Colo 80248

Berga Ullman Inc.
P.O. Box 918
North Adams
MA 01247

Happy Hands
3007 S. W. Marshall
Pendleton
Oreg 97180

International Old Lacers Inc.
124 West Irvington Place
Denver
Colo 80223-1539

The Lacemaker
23732-G. Bothell Hwy, SE
Bothell
WA 98021

Lace Place de Belgique
800 S. W. 17th Street
Boca Raton
FL 33432

Lacis
3163 Adeline Street
Berkeley
CA 94703

Robin's Bobbins
RTL Box 1736
Mineral Bluff
GA 30559-9736

Robin and Russ
Handweavers
533 North Adams Street
McMinnville
Oreg 97128

The Unique And Art
   Lace Cleaners
5926 Delman Boulevard
St Louis
MO 63112

Unicorn Books
Glimakra Looms 'n Yarns
   Inc.
1304 Scott Street
Petaluma
CA 94954-1181

Van Scriver Bobbin Lace
130 Cascadilla Park
Ithaca
NY 14850

The World in Stitches
82 South Street
Milford
NH 03055

Suppliers

Bryn Phillips
'Pantglas'
Cellan
Dyfed
Lampeter
SA48 8JD

D. H. Shaw
47 Zamor Crescent
Thruscroft
Rotherham
S. Yorks
S66 9QD

Sizelands
1 Highfield Road
Winslow
Bucks
MK10 3QU

Christine and David Springett
21 Hillmorton Road
Rugby
Warwickshire
CV22 5DF

Richard Viney
Unit 7
Port Royal Street
Southsea
Hants
PO5 4NP

George White
Delaheys Cottage
Thistle Hill
Knaresborough
N. Yorks

Books

Bridge Bookshop
7 Bridge Street
Bath
Avon
B82 4AS

Craft Bookcase
29 London Road
Sawbridgeworth
Herts
CM21 9EH

Christopher Williams
19 Morrison Avenue
Parkstone
Poole
Dorset
BH12 4AD

Silk embroidery and lace thread

Mulberry Silks
Unit 12A
Worcester Road Industrial Estate
Worcester Road
Chipping Norton
Oxfordshire
OX7 5XW

Doreen Holmes
39 Napier Road
Crowthorne
Berks
RG11 7EJ

E. and J. Piper
Silverlea
Flax Lane
Glemsford
Suffolk
CO10 7RS

Silk weaving yarn

Hilary Chetwynd
Kipping Cottage
Cheriton
Alresford
Hants
SQ24 0PW

Frames and mounts

Doreen Campbell
'Highcliff'
Bremilham Road
Malmesbury
Wilts

Matt coloured transparent adhesive film

Heffers Graphic Shop
26 King Street
Cambridge
CB1 1LN

United States of America

Arbor House
22 Arbor Lane
Roslyn Heights
NY 11577

Baltazor Inc
3262 Severn Avenue
Metairie
LA 7002

Beggars' Lace
P.O. Box 17263
Denver
Colorado 80217

The Lacemaker
23732-G Bothel Hwy SE
Bothel
WA 98021

Happy Hands
3007 S. W. Marshall
Pendleton
Oregon 97180

Lace Place de Belgique
800 S.W. 17th Street
Boca Raton
FL 33432

Lacis
2150 Stuart Street
Berkeley
California 94703

Robin's Bobbins
Rt1 Box 1736
Mineral Bluff
Georgia 30559

Robin and Russ Handweavers
533 North Adams Street
McMinnville
Oregon 97128

The Unique And Art Lace Cleaners
5926 Delman Boulevard
St Louis
Missouri 63112

Van Scriver Bobbin Lace
310 South Aurora Street
Ithaca
New York 14850

The World in Stitches
82 South Street
Milford
NH 03055

Australia

Dentelles Lace Supplies
3 Narrak Close
Jindalee
Queensland 4074

The Lacemaker
724A Riversdale Road
Camberwell
Victoria 3124

Spindle and Loom
Arcade 83
Longueville Road
Lane Cove
NSW 2066

Tulis Crafts
201 Avoca Street
Randwick
NSW 2031

Belgium

't Handwerkhuisje
Katelijnestraat 23
8000 Bruges
Belgium

Kantcentrum
Balstraat 14
8000 Bruges

Manufacture Belge de Dentelle
6 Galerie de la Reine
Galeries Royales St Hubert
1000 Bruxelles

France

Centre d'Initiation à la Dentelle du Puy
2 Rue Duguesclin
43000 Le Puy en Velay

A L'Econome
Anne-Marie Deydier
Ecole de Dentelle aux Fuseaux
10 rue Paul Chenavard
69001 Lyon

Rougier and Ple
13–15 bd des Filles de Calvaire
75003 Paris

West Germany

Der Fenster Laden
Berliner Str 8
D6483 Bad Soden
Salmunster

P. P. Hempel
Ortolanweg 34
1000 Berlin 47

Heikona De Ruijter
Kloeppelgrosshandel
Langer Steinweg 38
D4933 Blomberg

Holland

Blokker's Boektiek
Bronteeweg 4/4a
2101 AC Heemstede

Theo Brejaart
Postbus 5199
3008 AD Rotterdam

Magazinj De Vlijt
Lijnmarkt 48
Utrecht

Switzerland

Fadehax
Inh. Irene Solca
4105 Biel-Benken
Basel

New Zealand

Peter McLeavey
P.O. Box 69.007
Auckland 8

Sources of information

The Lace Guild
The Hollies
53 Audnam
Stourbridge
West Midlands
DY8 4AE

The Lace Society
Linwood
Stratford Road
Oversley
Alcester
Warwickshire
BY9 6PG

The Lacemakers' Circle
49 Wardwick
Derby
DE1 1HJ

The British College of Lace
21 Hillmorton Road
Rugby
Warwickshire
CV22 5DF

The English Lace School
Oak House
Woodbury
Nr. Exeter
EX5 1HP

International Old Lacers
President
Gunvor Jorgensen
366 Bradley Avenue
Northvale
NJ 076647
United States

United Kingdom Director of
International Old Lacers
S. Hurst
4 Dollius Road
London
N3 1RG

Guild of Needlelacers
Doreen Holmes (newsletter)
39 Napier Road
Crowthorne
Berks
RG11 7EJ

Ring of Tatters
Mrs Margaret Taylor
21 Buckstone Way
Leeds
LS17 5HE

Australian Lace Guild
29 Fife Street
Woodville South
South Australia 5011

New Zealand Lace Society
10 Lingard Street
Saint Albans
Christchurch 5
New Zealand

Bibliography

CLOSE, Eunice. *An Introduction to Needlepoint.* Wolverhampton, n. d.

DE DILLMONT, Thérèse. *The Complete DMC Encyclopedia of Needlework*, second edition. Running Press, Philadelphia, Pa., 1978

EARNSHAW, Pat. *Bobbin and Needlelaces: Identification and Care.* Batsford, 1983; paperback 1988.

HILLS, Ros. *Colour and Texture in Needlepoint Lace.* Dryad Press, 1987

HOLMES, Doreen. *Flowers in Needlepoint Lace.* Dryad Press, 1987

LOVESEY, Nenia. *The Technique of Needlepoint Lace.* Batsford, 1980

LOVESEY, Nenia. *Creative Design in Needlepoint Lace.* Batsford, 1983

LOVESEY, Nenia. *Introduction to Needlepoint Lace.* Batsford, 1985

LOVESEY, Nenia and BARLEY, Catherine. *Venetian Gros Point Lace.* Dryad Press, 1986

SUN, Ming-ju. *Oriental Floral Designs and Motifs for Artists, Needleworkers and Craftspeople.* Dover Publications Inc., New York, 1985

VOYSEY, Cynthia. *Needlelace in Photographs.* Batsford, 1987

WALRISCH-ROOT, Gineke. *Naaldkant Speels en Luchtig.* Cantecleer bv, de Bilt, 1982

WITHERS, Jean. *Mounting and Using Lace.* Dryad Press, 1986

Index

A
Acetate, adhesive 14, 19
Alençon-type mesh 72
Architect's linen 14,19

B
Backing (foundation) material 14, 18
Bars, buttonholed 119
Basic stitch 24, 27–30
Beads 89
Brooch, Venetian motif 111–114
Burano-type mesh 72

C
Chain of rings 110–111
Christmas tree decorations 86–91
    diamond 86–89
    round 89–91
Colour 116, 120, 121
Cordonnet 17, 20–24
    (see also individual motif instructions)
    branches 22–23
    butting threads 24
    couching 20–24
    ending 21–22
    interlocking 21, 22, 112
    joining 23
    starting 21
Cordonnette 17, 38–41
    (see also individual motif instructions)
    branches 39–40, 105–106
    'bridges' 106
    ending 40–41, 106
    joining laid threads 39
    padded (raised) 103–106
    scalloped (looped) 95–99
    starting 38–39
    wire in 89
Couronnes 106–111
    chain of rings 110–111
    disappearing 109
    scalloped 108
    simple ring 107–108
Curved shapes, working 112–113
Cushion-cover sampler 91–94

D
Daisy motif 43–65
    basic 43–60

inserted motif 61–62
    reduced size motif 62–65
Decreasing 38, 49
Design 19, 115–118

E
Ending off working thread 27, 39, 42
Enlarging a design 116
Equipment 13–16

F
Four-hole diamond 77–78

H
Hints on working 42
Holes 75–78
    four-hole diamond 77–78
    nine-hole diamond 78
    single 75–76
    slits 76

I
Increasing 38, 49
Insertion, of motif 61–62

J
Joining on, working thread 27, 39, 42, 47–48

L
Laid threads (see cordonnette)
Leaf motif 111–114
Loop picot, simple 100–101

M
Mat design 116, 117
Mounting, background 120–121

N
Needles, ball 13, 14, 26
Nine-hole diamond 78

P
Padding threads 103–106
Paperweight 61
Picots 99–102
    Alençon 101
    simple loop 100–101
    Venetian 101–102
Pillow 14–16

Index

Point de Gaze lace 65, 110
Preparation, general 18–20

R
Raised (padded) cordonnette 103–106
Reducing a design 116
Removal of lace from backing 41, 60
Ring stick 106, 107, 108

S
Samplers 25–26, 86–94
    basic 25–26
    Christmas decorations 86–91
    cushion cover 91–94
Scallops 95–99
    double layer 98
    simple 96–97, 99
    variations 98
Starting working thread 27, 39, 42
Stitches
    buttonholed wheel filling 85–86
    cinq point de Venise (shell) 81–82
    corded single Bruxelles 30–32, 118
    double Bruxelles 34–35
    double point de Venise 78–80
    lattice-type 36–37
    pea stitch and variations 72–75
    petit point de Venise 80
    single Bruxelles (net) 27–30

treble Bruxelles 35
twisted single Bruxelles and variations 66–72
wheel filling 83–85
whipped single Bruxelles 33–34
whipped twisted single Bruxelles 71–72

T
Threads 13, 14, 120
Tweezers 41, 60

U
Undoing stitches 42
Useful hints 42

V
Venetian Gros Point lace 95, 121
Venetian Gros Point leaf motif 111–114
Venetian picots 101–102

W
Washing 60
Wheel centre 54–56
Wheel centre, buttonholed 86
Whipping down, last rows 30, 35, 50
    (see also instructions for each stitch)
Wire 89

Y
Youghal lace 118